FIRE & SLICE

FIRE & SLICE

DELICIOUSLY SIMPLE RECIPES
FOR YOUR HOME PIZZA OVEN

RYLAND PETERS & SMALL
LONDON • NEW YORK

Designer Paul Stradling
Desk Editor Emily Calder
Head of Production Patricia Harrington
Creative Director Leslie Harrington
Editorial Director Julia Charles

Consultant Chef Theo Michaels
Indexer Vanessa Bird

First published in 2022 by Ryland Peters & Small
20–21 Jockey's Fields
London WC1R 4BW
and
341 E 116th St
New York, NY 10029

www.rylandpeters.com

10 9 8 7 6 5

Recipe collection compiled by Emily Calder.
Text © Valerie Aikman-Smith, Miranda Ballard, Fiona
Beckett, Ross Dobson, Clare Ferguson, Ursula Ferrigno,
Silvana Franco, Liz Franklin, Carol Hilker, Jennifer
Joyce, Jenny Linford, Jane Mason, Louise Pickford,
Isidora Popovic, Annie Rigg 2022.

Design and commissioned photography © Ryland
Peters & Small 2022 (see page 128 for picture credits).

ISBN: 978-1-78879-448-0

A CIP record for this book is available from the
British Library.
US Library of Congress Cataloging-in-Publication Data
has been applied for.

Printed and bound in China.

ACKNOWLEDGEMENTS

The Publishers wish to thank DeliVita for permission to
reproduce their images on pages 1, 8, 9, 10 and 11. DeliVita
is an innovative family-owned business that fuses British
craftsmanship with Italian style and heritage to handcraft
super luxe, wood-fired ovens in Yorkshire, UK. Find out
more at DeliVita.com. Thank you also to Theo Michaels,
for his generous advice on pizza-oven cooking.

NOTES

• Both British (metric) and American (imperial plus US
cups) are included in these recipes for your convenience;
however it is important to work with one set of
measurements and not alternate between the two.

• All spoon measurements are level unless otherwise
specified.

• Uncooked or partially cooked eggs should not be served
to the very old, frail, young children, pregnant women or
those with compromised immune systems.

• All pizza oven cooking instructions will vary based on the
model being used. Please check the information from your
provider. Results will vary.

• Whenever you're cooking with fire, remember that any
nearby surfaces will get hot, sparks can fly, and hot liquid
and fat may spill onto your skin. Use heatproof gloves, and
always have a first-aid kit and a fire extinguisher and fire
blanket, close to where you are cooking. And always
supervise children who are near a pizza oven.

CONTENTS

INTRODUCTION

The perfect way to feed the family, or entertain a crowd, a pizza night at home is becoming a much-loved institution. This collection of authentic, plus modern recipes, along with top tips on equipment and techniques, will help you get the very best pizzeria experience out of your pizza oven.

Originating in Naples to feed and fill the population cheaply, pizza has historically been considered a food of family and friendship. In a similar vein, focaccia were traditionally made in homes on the hot hearth where the embers had been, ready to tear and share as a communal treat. The modern revolutionization of the portable pizza oven means that you can get a piece of the action however you please, whether that be outside or inside, and with gas, wood, or wooden pellets. Whatever your pizza oven size, or chosen fuel, these recipes will help you to achieve authentic pizzas, with crispy charred crusts and bubbling cheese and perfectly risen focaccia.

You will find everything here from classic pizzas, to mini bite-size pizzette, and enjoy toppings ranging from the familiar Margherita and Pizza Fiorentina, to recipes that are a little more special, such as a Caramelized Red Onion Pizza with Capers & Olives and 'Nduja & Black Olive Tapenade. Or for the adventurous there is a Kimchi & Meatball pizza with Soy-lime Glaze. Want to really impress? Look to calzone recipes, such as Calzone Alla Parmigiana.

Focaccia gets its moment in the spotlight too – perfect served as a tear-and-share – choose from Roast Garlic & Rosemary, Fennel & Tomato, Potato & Olive, and more. And why not transform your kitchen into a buzzing pizzeria with freshly made pestos, chilli and garlic oils, mayos and classic Italian salads.

Forget greasy, overpriced pizzas from delivery chains, and cheap, chewy supermarket bases – you will never look back after discovering all the possibilities that your pizza oven holds. Embrace these delicious recipes to discover the unique results that come with cooking with good ingredients and fire, and take a little slice of Italy into your home. Bueno apetito!

EQUIPMENT & UTENSILS

Making pizza dough couldn't be easier, and when you become familiar with the process, you can guess the quantities by eye. To make really good pizza in a pizza oven, you will need a few basic items for handling dough and fire!

You should have a good selection of the usual suspects: **mixing bowls**, **measuring spoons**, **measuring jugs/pitchers**, **weighing scales** or **cup measures**; a good sharp **knife** or **pastry wheel** for cutting dough; a large **serrated knife** for cutting focaccia.

A very useful gadget is a **pastry scraper** which can be used as a knife, scoop and board scraper or cleaner. Scrapers come in all guises but they usually comprise a rectangular metal 'blade', one edge of which is covered by a wooden or plastic handle that fits into the palm of your hand.

If you are really serious about pizza making and want to make dough in quantity, an **electric food mixer** will take the pain out of mixing and kneading large batches of dough, although there's nothing quite as satisfying as hand-kneading a big, soft pillow of dough.

Clingfilm/plastic wrap is the modern alternative to a damp tea towel. This is used to cover a dough when it is rising to keep it moist and to stop the surface drying out and forming a crust, which can impair the rising. On its own it will stick to a dough, so lightly rub the dough with a little olive oil before covering the dough. Alternatively, cover the rising dough with a large, upturned mixing bowl.

A good, steady **work surface** at the right height is essential for energetic kneading. The surface should be able to cope with sticky dough, flour and olive oil and should be easy to clean.

A **flour sifter** or **shaker** is useful as it will limit the flour you sprinkle onto the dough and is always to hand. Alternatively, you can make do with a little bowl of extra flour on the side, for dusting.

An **olive-oil pourer** will allow you to drizzle small amounts of olive oil onto a pizza or into a dough. Some are cans with long spouts, and some neatly fit into the olive-oil bottle itself.

A **water spray** mists a dough with just enough water to keep it moist.

Pastry brushes are always handy, especially when brushing a calzone with oil or water and for brushing the edges of dough before sealing.

Cookie cutters will cut dough into smaller shapes for stuffing or filling.

A **pizza peel** is essential for launching and removing your pizzas in and out of the oven. Metal peels make for super easy turning and manoeuvring, whilst wooden peels double up as a serving board. Metal peels are great to scrape off any unwanted burnt bits without damaging the peel and they usually have a sharper edge.

A **cast iron skillet** for focaccia, and for pre-cooking other ingredients!

Fuel is vital – you can't make a pizza without a fire! Be it wood, pellets, or gas (for which you need a gas burner), make sure that you have the fuel you need and preheat your pizza oven with enough time.

Pizza wheels slice efficiently through a hot pizza without dragging off all the topping.

Heat resistant gloves are an essential – especially when handling a cast iron skillet.

PIZZA OVEN POINTERS

Using a pizza oven is quite different to cooking with a conventional oven —
you will need to bear in mind some tips to ensure both safety and success!

TIME

A hot pizza oven can cook authentic, crispy pizza in around 60 seconds – depending on your model. Keep a close eye on your pizza to ensure it doesn't burn!

TEMPERATURE

To get that charred, crispy crust, your oven needs to be hot, hot, hot! Preheating times vary depending on your oven and fuel, so make sure that it is switched on within plenty of time to reach approximately 500°C (932°F). You can often regulate the temperature on your oven depending on fuel amounts and how the vents are positioned — if recipes require a lower temperature, seek out instructions for your specific model.

VARIATIONS

Cooking times will vary depending on your fuel and specific oven – pizzas will have a standard cooking time of around 60 seconds at 500°C (932°F) but check your own model and provider for information too. Get to know your oven and your fuel – it is your friend!

ROTATION

Pizza ovens are hotter in some places than others, so for a consistently crispy base be sure to rotate your pizza every 20 seconds or so.

PRACTICE

Cooking with fire can take some getting used to, as can figuring out the temperature and hot spots of your oven. The area around the oven door is usually the coolest, whilst the areas closer to the fire will be hotter.

SAFETY

Pizza ovens can reach very high temperatures! This is what you want for perfectly cooked pizzas but do be careful when handling food and utensils in and out of the hot oven. Heat-resistant gloves will protect you, as will taking much care when cooking.

PIZZA POINTERS

Making pizza from scratch is both easy and fun, but there are a few things to bear in mind to make sure your dough is the best it can be!

YEAST
Whatever yeast you use, it needs moisture and warmth to develop. Make sure the liquid is at the correct temperature – too cold and the dough will rise slowly; too hot and you risk killing the yeast. When a recipe states 'hand-hot water', it should be between 40.5°C (105°F) and 46°C (115°F).

FLOUR
Using fine Italian '0' grade flour gives the best domestic results. Finer '00' grade is used by professionals and will not give a robust crust at home. Unbleached white bread flour, a mix of soft and hard wheats, will give a very good crust. If you are making dough in a hurry, warm the flour in the microwave for 10 seconds before adding the other ingredients. Always have surplus flour on hand to dust your dough, hands, rolling pin and work surface.

DOUGH
When making the dough, remember: the wetter the dough, the better the dough. A stiff, firm dough is difficult to knead and even more difficult to shape. It will have a poor texture and will not rise properly. If kneaded well, the stickiness soon disappears. Always have olive oil on hand for oiling clingfilm/plastic wrap, dough, bowls and pans, if required, to stop the dough from sticking.

KNEADING
If the dough sticks to your hands when kneading, stop and quickly wash your hands then dip them in a little flour to dry them. You will find the dough doesn't stick to clean hands. Kneading should stretch the dough and develop the elastic gluten in the flour – don't be shy in pulling and stretching the dough. Be careful not to over-knead your dough or it will become tough and brittle.

SHAPING
Starting off with a perfect round ball will make stretching the dough into a circle much easier. Shape each one into a smooth ball and place on a well-floured tea towel/dischcloth to rise. Dredge liberally all over with flour. When risen, flip the balls over onto a work surface (the flour will have stuck to the dough giving it a non-stick base) and roll out.

TOPPING
Remember that less is more – too much topping also stops the dough cooking and can make it mushy. The cardinal sin in pizza-making is to overwhelm perfectly made dough with too much topping. This can make it difficult to shoot into the oven and prevents it rising. If any topping drips down the side of the pizza, making it wet, it will not rise.

BASE

For the easiest way to handle your base in and out of the pizza oven, be sure to have a good pizza peel(s) on hand. Wooden peels are great for launching pizzas into the oven – and are a great serving plate! – but metal peels are better for rotating pizzas as they cook and removing them quickly and safely. Having both is ideal, but either will be fine!

BAKING

The best way to get a pizza into the oven is to roll the dough out on an even, floured surface, and slide this onto a lightly floured pizza peel. Take care when doing so to avoid tears. Always liberally dust your peel with flour then place the stretched dough base onto the peel before adding your toppings. If you try to put it on the peel after adding your toppings it always ends up a mess!

HERE AND NOW

Pizza bases and dough can be made in advance, but once you start adding toppings you need to cook it right away. If you add toppings too far in advance (anything more than a few minutes) the dough will get soggy and most likely break – so top and cook!

COOKING WITH KIDS

Top tip – precook the pizza bases for 30 seconds then once cooled give to the kids to take their time adding toppings before cooking again for a minute. This stops the bases going soggy while the kids have fun building their pizzas.

SERVING

Always serve a pizza as soon as it is cooked; slip it onto a wooden board and cut it using

a pizza wheel, as knives can drag the topping. Leave calzones to cool for 5 minutes before eating as they can burn the mouth!

EATING

Pizza is best eaten in the hand – the crust is there to act as a handle. In Naples, pizzas are folded in four and eaten like a huge sandwich in a paper napkin. Eating it with a knife and fork just sends it skimming across the plate!

A

B

D

E

G

H

BASIC PIZZA DOUGH

This will make the typical Neapolitan pizza – soft and chewy with a crisp crust or cornicione.

25 g/1 cake fresh/compressed yeast, 1 tablespoon/1 packet dried active baking yeast or 2 teaspoons fast-action/quick rising dried yeast

½ teaspoon caster/granulated sugar

250 ml/1 cup hand-hot water

500 g/4 cups unbleached white bread flour or Italian '0' flour, plus extra to dust

1 teaspoon fine sea salt

1 tablespoon extra virgin olive oil

MAKES 2 MEDIUM-CRUST PIZZAS, 25 CM/10 INCHES

In a medium bowl, cream the fresh/compressed yeast with the sugar and whisk in the hand-hot water (A). Leave for 10 minutes until frothy (B). For other yeasts, follow the manufacturer's instructions.

Sift the flour and salt into a large bowl and make a well in the centre. Pour in the yeast mixture (C), then the olive oil (D). Mix together with a round-bladed knife (E), then use your hands until the dough comes together. Tip out onto a lightly floured surface, wash and dry your hands, then knead briskly for 5–10 minutes until smooth, shiny and elastic (F) (Five minutes for warm hands, ten minutes for cold hands!). Don't add extra flour at this stage – a wetter dough is better. If you feel the dough is sticky, flour your hands, not the dough. The dough should be quite soft. If it is *really* too soft, knead in a little more flour.

To test if the dough is ready, roll it into a fat sausage, take each end in either hand, lift the dough up and stretch it outwards, gently wiggling it up and down – it should stretch out quite easily. If it doesn't, it needs more kneading. Shape the dough into a neat ball. Put in an oiled bowl, cover and leave to rise in a warm, draught-free place until doubled in size – about 1½ hours (G).

Uncover the dough, punch out the air, then tip out onto a lightly floured work surface. Divide into two and shape into smooth balls. Place the balls well apart on non-stick baking parchment, cover loosely and leave to rise for 60–90 minutes. Use as desired.

SALSA PIZZAIOLA

This is a key ingredient of pizza and gives it its distinctive flavour.
It is a speciality of Naples, but is quite common throughout Italy.
To acquire its concentrated, almost caramelized flavour, the tomatoes
must be fried over a lively heat.

8 tablespoons/½ cup olive oil
2 garlic cloves, chopped
1 teaspoon dried oregano
2 x 400-g/14-oz. cans
   chopped tomatoes (drained
   and juice reserved)
salt and freshly ground black
   pepper

MAKES ABOUT 400 ML/
1¾ CUPS

In a large, shallow pan, heat the oil almost to smoking point (a wok is good for this).

Standing back to avoid the spluttering, add the garlic, oregano and drained tomatoes, adding a little reserved canned tomato juice to loosen the mixture if the tomatoes start to stick to the base of the pan. Cook over fierce heat for 5–8 minutes or until the sauce is thick and glossy. Season.

Pass the sauce through a food mill (mouli) set over a bowl, to remove seeds and skin (C). You can put the smooth sauce back in the pan to reduce further if you like.

Ladle the sauce into the centre of the pizza base and spread it out in a circular motion with the back of a ladle (D).

A

B

C

D

A

B

C

BASIC FOCACCIA DOUGH

Focaccias are found in many different guises all over Italy, and can be thin and crisp, thick and soft, round or square. This basic one has been baked in a round pan, but it can be made in any shape you wish.

750 g/6⅓ cups Italian '00' flour or plain/all-purpose flour, plus extra to dust

25 g/1 cake fresh/compressed yeast, 1 tablespoon dried active baking yeast or 2 teaspoons fast-action/quick rising dried yeast

150 ml/⅔ cup extra virgin olive oil

425–500 ml/1¾–2 cups hand-hot water

sea salt flakes, to sprinkle

fresh rosemary needles (optional)

2 x 25-cm/10-inch cake pans

MAKES 2 FOCACCIAS, 25 CM/10 INCHES

Sift the flour and fine sea salt into a large bowl and make a well in the centre. Crumble in the fresh/compressed yeast. For other yeasts, follow the manufacturer's instructions. Pour in six tablespoons of the olive oil, then rub in the yeast until the mixture resembles fine breadcrumbs. Pour in the water and mix with your hands until the dough comes together.

Tip the dough out onto a floured surface, wash and dry your hands, and knead energetically for 10 minutes until smooth and elastic. The dough should be almost too soft to handle, but don't worry about that at this stage. Put it in a lightly oiled bowl, cover and leave to rise in a warm place until doubled in size – about 1½ hours.

Lightly oil two 25-cm/10-inch cake pans. Uncover the dough, punch out the air and divide in two. Shape each piece into a round ball on a lightly floured surface, roll out into two 25-cm/10-inch circles and place in the pans. Cover and leave to rise for 30 minutes.

Uncover the dough. Push your fingertips into the dough right down to the base of the pan (don't overdo it!), to make deep dimples all over the surface (A). The dough will deflate slightly. Drizzle very generously with about 80 ml/⅓ cup olive oil so that the dimples contain little pools of delicious oil (B). Top with little needles of rosemary leaves, if using, and a generous sprinkling of salt (C). Re-cover and leave the dough to rise to the top of the pans – about 30 minutes.

Preheat your pizza oven to 350°C (662°F).

Bake the focaccia in the preheated oven for 4–5 minutes, until golden-brown. Spoon over the remaining tablespoon of oil and sprinkle with salt.

Serve warm from the oven or at room temperature.

1

CLASSIC PIZZAS

SICILIAN-STYLE PIZZA MARGHERITA

The recipe for this basic pizza dough originated in Sicily. Using fresh yeast, a touch of lemon juice in the dough (usually made with special finely ground semolina flour for making bread, pasta and pizzas) makes it light and crisp. Adapt this recipe to ordinary plain/all-purpose flour and it works very well, but the crust is not as golden.

250 g/1¾ cups fine Italian semolina flour or plain/all-purpose flour

7 g/¼ oz. fresh/compressed yeast

1 tablespoon freshly squeezed lemon juice

1 tablespoon extra virgin olive oil

a pinch of sea salt

about 300 ml/1¼ cups warm water

PIZZA TOPPING

1 recipe Salsa Pizzaiola (page 16)

250-g/9-oz. ball fresh mozzarella cheese, thinly sliced

a handful of fresh basil leaves

extra virgin olive oil, to drizzle

salt and freshly ground black pepper, to season

a pizza peel

MAKES 2 THIN-CRUST PIZZAS, 23 CM/9 INCHES

Preheat your pizza oven to 500°C (932°F). Liberally dust your pizza peel with flour.

To make the dough, put the flour in a bowl, crumble the fresh yeast into the flour, add the lemon juice, olive oil and a generous pinch of salt, then add enough warm water to form a very soft dough. Transfer to a floured surface and knead for 10 minutes or until smooth and elastic. Put the dough in a clean, oiled bowl, cover and let rise for about 1 hour, until doubled in size.

Cut the dough in half and knead each half into a round. Pat or roll the rounds into 23-cm/9-inch circles, keeping the bases well floured. You will cook each pizza one at a time. Place the first stretched dough base on the pizza peel. Spread each pizza lightly with salsa pizzaiola, cover with sliced mozzarella cheese and season with salt and pepper. Let rise in a warm place for 10 minutes.

Working quickly, slide the pizza peel into your pizza oven. Bake for 60 seconds, rotating the pizza about every 20 seconds so that it bakes evenly and does not burn. The crust should appear golden, and the cheese melted and bubbling. Remove from the pizza oven, sprinkle with basil leaves and drizzle with extra virgin olive oil. Eat immediately.

FOUR CHEESE PIZZA

If you always reject the pizza Quattro Formaggi as being bland and indigestible, just try making it with top-quality Italian cheeses.

PIZZA DOUGH

150 g/1 cup strong white bread flour

125 g/1 cup minus 1 tablespoon Italian '00' flour

1 teaspoon sea salt

1 teaspoon fast-action/quick rising yeast

½ teaspoon caster/granulated sugar

2 tablespoons olive oil, plus extra to drizzle

about 175 ml/¾ cup hand-hot water

TOPPING

400 ml/1⅔ cups passata/strained tomatoes

150 g/5 oz. Pecorino Toscano cheese (rind removed), sliced

150 g/5 oz. Taleggio cheese (rind removed) or buffalo mozzarella cheese, sliced

90 g/3 oz. Gorgonzola piccante cheese, crumbled

30 g/⅓ cup freshly grated Parmesan cheese

a small handful of fresh oregano leaves

freshly ground black pepper, to season

a pizza peel

MAKES 2 PIZZAS

To make the pizza dough, sift the two flours into a bowl along with the salt, yeast and sugar. Mix together, then form a hollow in the centre. Add the olive oil and half the hand-hot water and stir to incorporate the flour. Gradually add as much of the remaining water as you need to pull the dough together. (It should take most of it – you need a wettish dough.) Turn the dough out onto a board and knead for 10 minutes until smooth and elastic, adding a little extra flour to prevent the dough sticking if necessary.

Put the dough into a lightly oiled bowl, cover and leave in a warm place until doubled in size, about 1–1¼ hours.

Preheat your pizza oven to 500°C (932°F). Liberally dust your pizza peel with flour.

Tip the dough out of the bowl and press down on it to knock out the air. Divide it in half. Pull and shape one piece of dough into a large circle, then place it on the pizza peel and push it out towards the edges of the peel. (It doesn't have to be a completely perfect circle!)

Spread half the passata over the top, then arrange half the cheeses over the top. Season with pepper. Repeat with the other piece of dough and the remaining cheese. Drizzle a little olive oil over the top of each pizza, and working quickly, slide the pizza peel into your pizza oven. Bake for 60 seconds, rotating about every 20 seconds so that it bakes evenly and does not burn. The dough will puff up and the cheese will be brown and bubbling.

Garnish the pizzas with oregano leaves and drizzle over a little more olive oil.

PIZZA MARINARA

This is the classic pizza and it is always made without mozzarella. According to Neapolitans, when anchovies are added, it is transformed into a Pizza Romana. Dried oregano is preferable to fresh, as it is much more fragrant, especially if you crush it between your fingers before sprinkling over the pizza. In Italy, wild oregano is sold in thick bunches, dries out in a matter of days and is rubbed straight off the bunch into whatever's cooking.

½ recipe Basic Pizza Dough (page 14), making just 1 ball of dough

3–4 tablespoons Pizzaiola Sauce (page 16)

2 or 3 very ripe tomatoes, sliced and deseeded

2 garlic cloves, thinly sliced

1 teaspoon dried oregano

extra virgin olive oil, to drizzle

salt and freshly ground black pepper, to season

a pizza peel

MAKES 1 MEDIUM-CRUST PIZZA, 25 CM/10 INCHES

Preheat your pizza oven to 500°C (932°F). Liberally dust your pizza peel with flour.

Uncover the dough, punch out the air and roll or pull into a 25-cm/10-inch circle onto a slightly floured surface. Place the stretched dough base on the pizza peel. Spread the pizzaiola sauce over the pizza base, leaving a 1-cm/½-inch rim around the edge. Scatter with the tomatoes and garlic, sprinkle with the dried oregano, drizzle with olive oil, then season.

Working quickly, slide the pizza peel into your pizza oven. Bake for 60 seconds, rotating the pizza about every 20 seconds so that it bakes evenly and does not burn. The crust should be golden. Remove from the oven and drizzle with olive oil. Eat immediately.

PIZZA ARRABIATA

This is quite a substantial pizza, and can be as fiery and angry (arrabiata) as you like – it's up to you how much chilli you put in. This is delicious made with fresh Italian sausage meat, but you could use thick slices of salame piccante or even a hot merguez or chorizo. Chilled beer is an essential accompaniment!

½ recipe Basic Pizza Dough (page 14), making just 1 ball of dough

50–75 g/2–3 oz. buffalo mozzarella cheese or cow's milk mozzarella cheese (*fior di latte*)

200 g/about 6 fresh plum tomatoes, halved

150 g/5 oz. fresh spicy sausage, sliced or removed from the skin and crumbled

50 g/2 oz. Peppadew peppers

½ teaspoon fennel seeds

dried chilli/hot red pepper flakes, to taste

Chilli/Chile Oil (page 103) or extra virgin olive oil, to drizzle

salt and freshly ground black pepper, to season

a pizza peel

MAKES 1 MEDIUM-CRUST PIZZA, 25 CM/10 INCHES

Preheat your pizza oven to 400°C (752°F). Liberally dust your pizza peel with flour.

Lightly squeeze any excess moisture out of the mozzarella, then slice or chop into cubes.

Uncover the dough, punch out the air and roll or pull into a 25-cm/10-inch circle directly onto a lightly floured surface. Place the stretched dough base on the pizza peel. Arrange the tomatoes over the pizza base, leaving a 1-cm/½-inch rim around the edge. Scatter with sausage, then the Peppadew peppers, then the mozzarella. Sprinkle with fennel seeds and chilli flakes, then season.

Working quickly, slide the pizza peel into your pizza oven. Bake for 60–90 seconds, depending on the strength of your pizza oven, rotating the pizza about every 20 seconds so that it bakes evenly and does not burn. The crust should be golden and the cheese melted but still white. Remove from the oven and drizzle with chilli oil. Eat immediately.

PIZZA BIANCA

Neapolitans naturally call pizza without tomatoes pizza bianca ('white pizza'). All the flavour comes from the cheese, so it has to be the finest buffalo mozzarella. This tends to be quite wet, so squeeze out any watery whey before slicing it. Try adding sage to the pizza – its muskiness beautifully complements the milky mozzarella.

½ recipe Basic Pizza Dough (page 14), making just 1 ball of dough
100 g/3½ oz. buffalo mozzarella cheese or cow's milk mozzarella cheese (*fior di latte*)
a handful of small fresh sage leaves
extra virgin olive oil, to drizzle
salt and freshly ground black pepper, to season

a pizza peel

MAKES 1 MEDIUM-CRUST PIZZA, 25 CM/10 INCHES

Preheat your pizza oven to 500°C (932°F). Liberally dust your pizza peel with flour.

Lightly squeeze any excess moisture out of the mozzarella cheese, then slice it and put it on kitchen paper/paper towels for 5 minutes to absorb any remaining moisture.

Uncover the dough, punch out the air and roll or pull into a 25-cm/10-inch circle directly onto a lightly floured surface. Place the stretched dough base on the pizza peel. Arrange the mozzarella evenly over the pizza base, leaving a 1-cm/½-inch rim around the edge. Scatter the sage over the cheese, then season and drizzle with olive oil.

Working quickly, slide the pizza peel into your pizza oven. Bake for 60 seconds, rotating the pizza about every 20 seconds so that it bakes evenly and does not burn. The crust will be golden and the cheese melted and bubbling. Remove from the oven and sprinkle with freshly ground black pepper. Eat immediately.

PIZZA FIORENTINA

Spinach and egg pizzas are a favourite in pizza restaurants everywhere, and you can easily make them at home. It doesn't matter if the yolk is a bit hard, but make sure it goes onto the pizza whole.

1 recipe Basic Pizza Dough
(page 14)

350 g/13 oz. baby spinach
leaves, destalked

1 tablespoon butter

2 garlic cloves, crushed

1–2 tablespoons olive oil

½ recipe Salsa Pizzaiola
(page 16)

150 g/5 oz. mozzarella cheese,
drained and thinly sliced

4 eggs

50 g/½ cup finely grated
fontina cheese or Gruyère
cheese

salt and freshly ground black
pepper, to season

a pizza peel

MAKES 4 SMALL DEEP CRUST
PIZZAS, 17 CM/7 INCHES

Preheat your pizza oven to 400°C (752°F). Liberally dust your pizza peel with flour.

Wash the spinach thoroughly and put into a large saucepan. Cover with a lid and cook for 2–3 minutes, until the spinach wilts. Drain well and, when the spinach is cool enough to handle, squeeze out any excess water with your hands.

Melt the butter in a frying pan/skillet and cook the garlic for 1 minute. Add the drained spinach and cook for a further 3–4 minutes. Add salt and pepper to taste.

Divide the dough into four, put on a lightly floured surface and roll out each piece to about 17 cm/7 inches in diameter. Place the stretched dough base on the pizza peel. Brush with a little oil and spoon over the tomato sauce. Put the spinach on the bases, leaving a space in the middle for the egg. Put the mozzarella cheese on top of the spinach, drizzle with a little more oil and season with salt and plenty of black pepper.

Working quickly, slide the pizza peel into your pizza oven. Bake for 60 seconds, rotating after about 30 seconds. Remove the pizza from the oven. Crack the egg into the middle of the pizza. Top with the fontina cheese or Gruyère cheese. Place in the front (cooler) part of the oven for a further 60 seconds, until the base is crisp and golden and the eggs have just set. Serve immediately.

PANCETTA PIZZA

For this recipe use very thinly sliced smoked pancetta (the Italian equivalent of streaky bacon, made from salt-cured pork belly). Pancetta comes in many forms: in whole cured slabs (with or without herbs and spices), smoked or unsmoked, or rolled up for slicing thinly, aged or not. The choice is endless and varies from region to region. Outside Italy, you can buy the smoked slab with rind, ready-sliced smoked or rolled unsmoked pancetta. Combined with Fiery Red Pesto (page 107), this is incredible!

1 recipe Basic Pizza Dough (page 14)

6 tablespoons Fiery Red Pesto (page 107)

24 thin slices pancetta or thin streaky bacon

extra virgin olive oil, to drizzle

salt and freshly ground black pepper, to season

a pizza peel

MAKES 1 MEDIUM-CRUST RECTANGULAR PIZZA, APPROXIMATELY 20 X 40 CM/8 X 16 INCHES

Preheat your pizza oven to 500°C (932°F). Liberally dust your pizza peel with flour.

Uncover the dough, punch out the air and roll or pull into a rectangle, about 20 cm/8 inches wide and as long as your peel will take (you can always make two shorter ones). Roll the dough directly onto a lightly floured surface. Place the stretched dough base on the pizza peel.

Spread the red pesto over the pizza base, leaving a 1-cm/½-inch rim around the edge. Lay the strips of pancetta widthways across the pizza – they should be almost the same width as the dough. Season and drizzle with oil.

Working quickly, slide the pizza peel into your pizza oven. Bake for 60 seconds, rotating the pizza halfway through so that it bakes evenly and does not burn. The crust will be golden and the pancetta crisp. Remove from the oven and drizzle with olive oil. Cut into fingers and eat immediately.

PIZZA PICCANTE

This contains all the heat of southern Italy. Provolone piccante, originally from Campania, is a sharp, aged cow's milk cheese often found in a globe shape and usually covered in a waxed rind. It also makes a delicious sandwich with fresh tomato, dried oregano and a drizzle of olive oil.

½ recipe Basic Pizza Dough (page 14), making just 1 ball of dough

4 tablespoons Pizzaiola Sauce (page 16)

50 g/2 oz. buffalo mozzarella cheese or cow's milk mozzarella cheese (*fior di latte*)

3 large garlic cloves, thinly sliced

50 g/2 oz. *provolone piccante* cheese, thinly sliced

2 fat red fresh chillies/chiles (or more), thinly sliced

extra virgin olive oil, to drizzle

Chilli/Chile Oil (page 103), to drizzle

salt and freshly ground black pepper, to season

a pizza peel

MAKES 1 MEDIUM-CRUST PIZZA, 25 CM/10 INCHES

Preheat your pizza oven to 500°C (932°F). Liberally dust your pizza peel with flour.

Lightly squeeze any excess moisture out of the mozzarella, then slice it and leave the slices on kitchen paper for 5 minutes to absorb any remaining moisture.

Uncover the dough, punch out the air and roll or pull into a 25-cm/10-inch circle directly onto a lightly floured surface. Place the stretched dough base on the pizza peel. Spread the pizzaiola sauce over the pizza base, leaving a 1-cm/½-inch rim around the edge. Scatter the garlic over the top. Arrange the provolone and mozzarella on top and scatter with the chillies. Season well with plenty of freshly ground black pepper and drizzle with olive oil.

Working quickly, slide the pizza peel into your pizza oven. Bake for 60 seconds, rotating the pizza about every 20 seconds so that it bakes evenly and does not burn. The crust will be golden, and the cheese melted and bubbling. Remove from the pizza oven and drizzle with the chilli oil. Eat immediately.

2

SOMETHING SPECIAL

GARLIC MUSHROOM PIZZA

This makes a change from the normal scattering of token sliced mushrooms: here we have fresh mushrooms in all their glory, under a crispy garlicky topping of breadcrumbs and Parmesan. Don't use white mushrooms for this – they often have little or no taste at all. Chestnut/cremini or other large, dark open mushrooms are ideal.

½ recipe Basic Pizza Dough (page 14), making just 1 ball of dough

50–75 g/2–3 oz. buffalo mozzarella cheese or cow's milk mozzarella cheese (*fior di latte*)

50 g/½ cup fresh breadcrumbs

30 g/¼ cup freshly grated Parmesan cheese

4 garlic cloves, finely chopped

4 tablespoons chopped fresh flat-leaf parsley

30 g/2 tablespoons butter, melted

about 12 medium chestnut/cremini mushrooms

extra virgin olive oil, to drizzle

salt and freshly ground black pepper, to season

a pizza peel

MAKES 1 MEDIUM-CRUST PIZZA, 25 CM/10 INCHES

Preheat your pizza oven to 350°C (662°F). Liberally dust your pizza peel with flour.

Lightly squeeze any excess moisture out of the mozzarella, then slice or chop into cubes. Mix the breadcrumbs with the Parmesan cheese, garlic and parsley, then stir in the melted butter. Lightly fill the cavities of the mushrooms with the breadcrumb mixture.

Uncover the dough, punch out the air and roll or pull into a 25-cm/10-inch circle directly onto a lightly floured surface. Place the stretched dough base on the pizza peel. Arrange the mozzarella over the pizza base leaving a 2-cm/1-inch rim around the edge. Make indents for each mushroom in the pizza. Drizzle with olive oil and season.

Working quickly, open the oven door and slide in the pizza peel. Bake for 30 seconds, just enough to set the base slightly. Remove from the oven and place the stuffed mushrooms in the indents, sprinkling any remaining breadcrumbs over the finished pizza. Bake for a further 60 seconds or so, rotating halfway through, until the crust is golden, the cheese melted and the mushrooms tender and bubbling. Remove from the oven and drizzle with olive oil. Eat immediately.

CARAMELIZED RED ONION PIZZA WITH CAPERS & OLIVES

With no hint of tomato sauce, this is a succulent pizza where the onions are cooked until soft and caramelized, before being spread on the pizza on top of the mozzarella. Olives, capers and anchovies add savouriness to the sweet onions. You may leave out the anchovies and add tuna or sardines instead.

1 recipe Basic Pizza Dough (page 14), dividing the dough into 6–8 balls, as desired

1 kg/2¼ lb. red onions, finely sliced

freshly squeezed juice of 1 lemon

4 tablespoons olive oil, plus extra to drizzle

2 teaspoons dried oregano

1 ball of fresh mozzarella, drained and thinly sliced

2 tablespoons freshly grated Parmesan cheese

12 anchovy fillets in oil, drained (optional)

15 black olives, pitted

2 tablespoons capers in salt, washed and drained

salt and freshly ground black pepper, to season

a pizza peel

MAKES 6–8 SMALL PIZZAS, DEPENDING ON SIZE

Preheat your pizza oven to 500°C (932°F). Liberally dust your pizza peel with flour.

Toss the onions in the lemon juice to coat them thoroughly. Heat the oil in a large, shallow saucepan and add the onions. Cook over a gentle heat for about 10 minutes, stirring occasionally, until they are beginning to colour. Stir in the dried oregano.

Uncover the dough balls, punch out the air and roll or pull each one into thin circles directly onto a lightly floured surface. Place these a few at a time onto the pizza peel to cook.

Cover the pizza bases with the mozzarella cheese leaving a 1-cm/½-inch rim around the edge. Top with the onions and sprinkle with the Parmesan cheese. Scatter the anchovy fillets, olives and capers over the top. Drizzle with olive oil, then season, but don't use too much salt as the capers will be salty.

Working quickly, open the oven door, and slide in the pizza peel. Bake for 60 seconds, rotating halfway through, or until the crust is golden. Remove from the oven and drizzle with olive oil. Eat immediately.

PRAWN/SHRIMP & TOMATO PIZZA

Using the plumpest raw prawns/shrimp you can find will ensure that they don't toughen up through over-cooking.

½ recipe Basic Pizza Dough (page 14), making just 1 ball of dough

3–4 tablespoons Pizzaiola Sauce (page 16)

3 garlic cloves, sliced thinly

½ teaspoon dried chilli/hot red pepper flakes

10–12 medium raw prawns/shrimp

200 g/1 cup very ripe cherry tomatoes or any other very tasty small tomatoes

a handful of fresh flat-leaf parsley, roughly chopped

extra virgin olive oil, to drizzle

salt and freshly ground black pepper, to season

lemon wedges, to serve

a pizza peel

MAKES 1 MEDIUM-CRUST PIZZA, 25 CM/10 INCHES

Preheat your pizza oven to 400°C (752°F). Liberally dust your pizza peel with flour.

Uncover the dough, punch out the air and roll or pull into a 25-cm/10-inch circle directly onto a lightly floured surface. Place the stretched dough base on the pizza peel. Spread the pizzaiola sauce over the pizza base, leaving a 1-cm/½-inch rim around the edge. Scatter with the garlic, chilli flakes, prawns and tomatoes. Season.

Working quickly, slide the pizza peel into your pizza oven. Bake for 90 seconds, rotating the pizza about every 30 seconds so that it bakes evenly and does not burn. The crust should be golden. Remove from the oven, scatter with the parsley and drizzle with olive oil. Eat immediately with the lemon wedges for squeezing over the pizza.

PIZZA WITH ARTICHOKES & MOZZARELLA

Artichokes preserved in oil for antipasti are perfect for pizza-making as the delicious oil they are soaked in means they won't dry out during cooking. You can also make this with smoked mozzarella and it is equally delicious.

½ recipe Basic Pizza Dough (page 14), making just 1 ball of dough

100 g/3½ oz. buffalo mozzarella cheese or cow's milk mozzarella cheese (*fior di latte*)

100 g/3½ oz. artichokes preserved in oil (or grilled artichokes from a deli)

1–2 garlic cloves, finely chopped

2 tablespoons extra virgin olive oil, plus extra to drizzle

6–8 juicy black olives, pitted

2 tablespoons fresh flat-leaf parsley, roughly chopped

salt and freshly ground black pepper, to season

a pizza peel

MAKES 1 MEDIUM-CRUST PIZZA, 25 CM/10 INCHES, OR 2 SMALL PIZZAS (AS SHOWN)

Preheat your pizza oven to 500°C (932°F). Liberally dust your pizza peel with flour.

Lightly squeeze any excess moisture out of the mozzarella, then slice it and leave the slices on kitchen paper/paper towels for 5 minutes to absorb any remaining moisture. Cut the artichokes into quarters and toss them with the garlic and olive oil.

Uncover the dough, punch out the air and roll or pull into a 25-cm/10-inch circle directly onto a lightly floured surface. Place the stretched dough base on the pizza peel. Arrange the mozzarella evenly over the pizza base, leaving a 1-cm/½-inch rim around the edge. Scatter the artichoke and olives over the mozzarella, then season and drizzle with olive oil.

Working quickly, slide the pizza peel into your pizza oven. Bake for 60 seconds, rotating the pizza about every 20 seconds so that it bakes evenly and does not burn. The crust will be golden and the cheese melted and bubbling. Remove from the oven and sprinkle the parsley and freshly ground black pepper over the top. Eat immediately.

PEAR, PECORINO & TALEGGIO PIZZA WITH HONEY & SAGE

This is a sort of new-wave pizza, and very popular in Italian city pizzerias. Soft, buttery Taleggio cheese, made in the valleys and mountains of Lombardy and the Valtellina, melts and runs very quickly, so make sure it's not near the edge of the pizza. Ripe, juicy pear is the perfect foil for this cheese, and don't leave out the sage – it's integral to the flavour.

½ recipe Basic Pizza Dough (page 14), making just 1 ball of dough

2 tablespoons extra virgin olive oil, plus extra to drizzle

125 g/4 oz. Taleggio cheese (rind removed), cubed

1 very ripe pear, cored and thinly sliced

12–15 small fresh sage leaves

50 g/½ cup freshly grated pecorino cheese

1 tablespoon runny honey

salt and freshly ground black pepper, to season

a pizza peel

MAKES 1 MEDIUM-CRUST PIZZA, 25 CM/10 INCHES

Preheat your pizza oven to 500°C (932°F). Liberally dust your pizza peel with flour.

Uncover the dough, punch out the air and roll or pull into a 25-cm/10-inch circle directly onto a lightly floured surface. Place the stretched dough base on the pizza peel. Rub the pizza base with the olive oil and scatter over the Taleggio cheese. Arrange the pears over this, then the sage and pecorino cheese. Drizzle with the honey, then season as desired and drizzle with a little more olive oil.

Working quickly, slide the pizza peel into your pizza oven. Bake for 60 seconds, rotating the pizza about every 20 seconds so that it bakes evenly and does not burn. The crust will be golden and the cheese melted and bubbling. Sprinkle with freshly ground black pepper and eat immediately.

SPINACH, ARTICHOKE & GOATS' CHEESE PIZZA

This pizza has a mixture of green vegetables and mild, creamy goats' cheese that make it a delicious and masterful way of enjoying pizza that is both packed with flavour yet light, fresh and nutritious.

½ recipe for Basic Pizza Dough (page 14), making just 1 ball of dough

125 ml/½ cup Pizzaiola Sauce (page 16)

250 g/2 cups fresh mozzarella cheese, grated

400g/14-oz. can quartered artichoke hearts, drained and halved

60–90 g/2–3 cups baby spinach leaves, destalked

1 large ripe tomato, cut into large chunks

60 g/½ cup small balls or sliced rounds of soft white goats' cheese

a large handful of fresh basil leaves

dried chilli/hot red pepper flakes, to taste (optional)

salt and freshly ground black pepper, to season

a pizza peel

MAKES 1 THIN-CRUST PIZZA, 30 CM/12 INCHES

Preheat your pizza oven to 400°C (752°F). Liberally dust your pizza peel with flour. Uncover the dough, punch out the air and roll or pull into a round of about 30 cm/12 inches directly onto a lightly floured surface. Place the stretched dough base on the pizza peel. Spread the pizzaiola sauce on the crust. Sprinkle half of the mozzarella on top.

Scatter spinach leaves evenly over the crust then top with the artichokes and tomato slices. Sprinkle the remaining mozzarella cheese on top (the cheese will hold it together).

Arrange small balls/slices of goat cheese over the top and add some torn fresh basil to the top of the pizza.

Working quickly, slide the pizza peel into your pizza oven. Bake for 90 seconds, rotating the pizza about every 30 seconds so that it bakes evenly and does not burn. Sprinkle some chilli flakes over the top, if using, season and serve immediately.

PIZZA CALABRESE

A poem of Calabrian flavours on a pizza! Try tracking down rapini, known for its earthy, slightly bitter taste and beloved by Italian and Spanish cooks. It is not related to broccoli at all but is related to the turnip. In different parts of Italy, it is confusingly known as cima di rape ('turnip tops'), broccoli rabe, friarielli, broccoletti, broccoli friarelli, broccoli di rape, rapi or rapini. (USA broccoli raab, rabe, rab, rape). However if not available, turnip or beetroot/beet tops are a good substitute, then purple sprouting broccoli, tenderstem broccoli and last of all, normal broccoli.

½ recipe Basic Pizza Dough (page 14), making just 1 ball of dough

3–4 tablespoons Pizzaiola Sauce (page 16)

50 g/2 oz. purple sprouting broccoli or other broccoli (see recipe introduction), sliced in half lengthways

100 g/3½ oz. 'nduja (spicy Calabrian sausage)

1 teaspoon dried oregano

5–7 wrinkly black olives, pitted

1 egg

extra virgin olive oil, to drizzle

salt and freshly ground black pepper, to season

a pizza peel

MAKES 1 MEDIUM-CRUST PIZZA (25 CM/10 INCHES)

Preheat your pizza oven to 400°C (752°F). Liberally dust your pizza peel with flour.

Blanch the broccoli in boiling salted water for 30 seconds, then drain and refresh in cold water.

Uncover the dough, punch out the air and roll or pull into a 25-cm/10-inch circle directly onto a lightly floured surface. Place the stretched dough base on the pizza peel. Spread the pizzaiola sauce over the pizza base, leaving a 1-cm/⅜-inch rim around the edge. Spoon over the 'nduja. Drain the broccoli and scatter over the pizza. Sprinkle with the dried oregano, then the olives, drizzle with olive oil, then season.

Working quickly, slide the pizza peel into your pizza oven. Bake for 60 seconds, rotating after about 30 seconds. Remove the pizza from the oven. Crack the egg into the middle (if using). Place in the front (cooler) part of the oven for a further 60 seconds, until until the egg is just cooked and the crust is golden. Remove from the oven and drizzle with olive oil. Eat immediately.

KIMCHI & MEATBALL PIZZA
WITH SOY-LIME GLAZE

An Asian-inspired version of a meatball pizza. There are a lot of ingredients but it's worth it for a special treat!

1 recipe Basic Pizza Dough
(page 14)
200 g/7 oz. smoked firm tofu,
grated
12 pre-cooked Asian-style mini
meatballs from your deli
counter

KIMCHI SALAD
1 small cucumber
1 large carrot
3 spring onions/scallions
25 g/1 oz. grated fresh ginger
2 garlic cloves, thinly sliced
2 teaspoons caster/granulated
sugar
1–2 teaspoons fish sauce
1–2 teaspoons soy sauce
2 teaspoons rice vinegar
6–8 sprigs fresh coriander/
cilantro

SOY-LIME GLAZE
4 tablespoons soy sauce
2 teaspoons sesame oil
4 tablespoons freshly
squeezed lime juice
2 tablespoons soft brown
sugar

a pizza peel

MAKES 2 THIN-CRUST PIZZAS
(35 CM/14 INCHES)

Make the kimchi salad the day before if possible. Using a potato peeler, shave long strips from the cucumber avoiding the wet seeds. Do the same with the carrot and shred the spring onions. Mix the ginger, garlic, sugar, fish sauce, soy sauce and rice vinegar together in the bottom of a medium bowl. Throw in the vegetables and toss well to coat. Cover and refrigerate for as long as possible.

Preheat your pizza oven to 500°C (932°F). Liberally dust your pizza peel with flour.

For the soy–lime glaze, stir together the soy sauce, sesame oil, lime juice and sugar with 4 tablespoons of water in a small saucepan and boil for 2–3 minutes until slightly thickened. Set aside.

Uncover the dough, punch out the air and roll or pull into two 35-cm/14-inch circles directly onto a lightly floured surface. You will cook these pizzas one at a time. Place the first stretched dough base on the pizza peel. Scatter the tofu over the pizza base, leaving a 1-cm/⅜-inch rim around the edge. Arrange the meatballs on top, then working quickly, slide the pizza peel into your pizza oven. Bake for 60 seconds, rotating the pizza about every 20 seconds so that it bakes evenly and does not burn.

The crust will be golden when ready. Remove from the pizza oven, drizzle with the glaze then divide the kimchi between the two pizzas, piling high. Finish with the coriander sprigs, and eat immediately.

WHEAT-FREE PIZZA
WITH ROASTED VEGETABLES

*This wheat-free pizza is very good, but don't expect a pizza-like dough.
It starts life as a batter and when baked, becomes chewy and sponge-like
on the inside, with a crisp crust. The recipe uses a gluten-free flour and
is perfect for those who can't eat wheat but still crave that unique
pizza experience.*

**3 tablespoons each milk
and water, mixed
together and warmed**

**¾ teaspoon freshly squeezed
lemon juice**

**2 tablespoons olive oil,
plus extra to drizzle**

1 egg

½ teaspoon salt

**225 g/1¾ cups gluten-free
white bread flour, such
as Dove's Farm or Bob's
Red Mill**

**1 teaspoon fast-action/quick
rising dried yeast**

**½ aubergine/eggplant, thinly
sliced**

**1 small red (bell) pepper,
deseeded and cut into
very thin strips**

**1 small courgette/zucchini,
thinly sliced**

**75 g/2½ oz. fresh mozzarella
cheese, drained and cubed
(optional)**

**salt and freshly ground black
pepper, to season**

a cast-iron skillet, greased

MAKES 1 PIZZA, 23 CM/
9 INCHES

Preheat your pizza oven to 400°C (752°F). Preheat the cast-iron
skillet in the oven.

Make the batter. Whisk the warm (not hot) milk and
water, the lemon juice, olive oil, egg and salt together.
Beat in the flour and yeast and mix until well combined. Leave
to rise in a warm place for about 20 minutes or until puffy.
Place in the preheated cast-iron skillet, making sure it is less
than 1 cm/½ inch thick and slide this into the pizza oven for
two minutes to set the base.

Quickly remove from the oven and scatter with the vegetables
and mozzarella cheese (if using). Season well, drizzle with olive
oil and return to the oven for a further 2 minutes until the
vegetables are sizzling and the pizza has slightly shrunk from
the edges, turning occasionally so that the pizza cooks evenly.
Cut into wedges and serve hot.

TRIPLE TOMATO PIZZA

This simple recipe offers a classic combination of flavours and makes four large pizzas to feed a crowd!

500 g/4 cups strong bread flour

1 teaspoon caster/granulated sugar

1 teaspoon salt

1 teaspoon fast-action/quick rising dried yeast

300 ml/1¼ cups lukewarm water

2 tablespoons olive oil

PIZZA TOPPING

300 ml/1¼ cups passata/ strained tomatoes

8 sun-dried or sun-blush tomatoes in oil, chopped

8 cherry tomatoes, halved

2 balls fresh mozzarella cheese, chopped

8 anchovy fillets in oil (each about 10 g/⅓ oz.)

fresh basil leaves, to garnish

salt and freshly ground black pepper, to season

a pizza peel

MAKES 4

First, make the pizza dough. Mix together the flour, sugar, salt and yeast. Gradually, pour in the lukewarm water and the oil, forming a sticky dough. Turn out onto a lightly floured surface and knead until smooth and elastic. Put the dough into a lightly oiled bowl, cover with and set aside in a warm place to rise for an hour.

Preheat your pizza oven to 500°C (932°F). Liberally dust your pizza peel with flour.

Break down the pizza dough and roll out on a lightly floured surface to form four pizza bases.

You will bake these one at a time. Place the stretched dough base on the pizza peel. Spread with passata, leaving a rim of plain dough around the edge. Top each pizza with the sun-dried tomatoes, cherry tomatoes, mozzarella cheese and anchovy fillets.

Working quickly, slide the pizza peel into your pizza oven. Bake for 60 seconds, rotating the pizza about every 20 seconds so that it bakes evenly and does not burn. The mozzarella cheese will be melted and the dough golden. Sprinkle with basil leaves, season and serve at once.

ALPINE PIZZA

These squashy, ovalish pizza-like flat-breads are typically made with just about any flour. They are rolled roughly and topped with various simple things like quark (a kind of soft cheese), speck (a kind of bacon) and sliced onions.

300 g/2⅓ cups strong bread flour
1.5 g/¾ teaspoon fast-action/ quick rising dried yeast
180 g/¾ cup water
3 g/¾ teaspoon salt

Choose from the following toppings:

quark cheese (if you cannot get this, mash some cottage cheese and feta into a spreadable paste)
cubed bacon, speck, lardons, pancetta, country ham
thinly sliced onion or shallots
dried mixed herbs
dried mushrooms
anything you would put on a pizza that you can get in the mountains

a pizza peel

MAKES 6 SMALL PIZZAS

Preheat your pizza oven to 400°C (752°F). Liberally dust your pizza peel with flour.

Put all the ingredients in a big bowl and mix them together. Tip onto a lightly floured furface and knead well for 10 minutes.

Pop the kneaded dough back into the bowl and cover. Allow to rest for 1–2 hours until it has doubled in size.

Divide the dough into six equal portions. One by one, roll them into ovals about 0.5 cm/¼ inch thick on a lightly floured surface and using a floury rolling pin. Prick each one with a fork several times so it does not puff up in the oven. Place the stretched dough bases on the pizza peel. Spread quark over the pizza bases, leaving a bare border. Top with the toppings of your choice.

Working quickly, slide the pizza peel into your pizza oven. Bake for 60–90 seconds, rotating the pizza about every 30 seconds so that it bakes evenly and does not burn. Eat immediately.

3

PIZZETTE & CALZONES

PIZZA DOUGH

1½ level teaspoons fast-action/quick rising dried yeast

250 g/1¾ cups plain/all-purpose flour

½ teaspoon salt

5 tablespoons olive oil

175 ml/⅔ cup hand-hot water

TOPPINGS

1 small aubergine/eggplant, thinly sliced

1 onion, thinly sliced

a pinch of fresh thyme leaves

4 generous teaspoons sun-dried tomato paste

75 g/½ cup cherry tomatoes, quartered

125 g/4 oz. dolcelatte or Gorgonzola cheese, crumbled

8 pepperoni slices

a handful of black olives, pitted

100 g/3½ oz. fresh mozzarella cheese, diced

2 teaspoons Classic Green Pesto (page 104) or store-bought fresh pesto

2 canned artichoke hearts, sliced

2 tablespoons semi-dried tomatoes

a handful of wild rocket/arugula

salt and freshly ground black pepper, to season

fresh basil leaves, to garnish

a pizza peel

MAKES 4 PIZZETTE,
15 CM/6 INCHES

MIXED PIZZETTE PLATTER

This selection of mini pizzas has four deliciously different toppings: aubergine/eggplant and dolcelatte; pepperoni, mozzarella and olives; artichoke, semi-dried tomato and pesto; and sautéed onions with dolcelatte.

To make the pizza dough, mix together the flour, yeast and salt in a large bowl. Add 2 tablespoons of the olive oil and the water and mix to a soft dough. Lightly dust the work surface with flour, tip the dough out of the bowl and knead for 5 minutes, or until smooth and elastic. Shape the dough into a neat, smooth ball, return to the bowl and cover. Leave in a warm place for 1 hour, or until doubled in size.

Heat 2 tablespoons of the oil in a frying pan/skillet and fry the aubergine on both sides until golden, then remove from the heat. In another pan, heat the remaining olive oil and gently fry the onion until very tender and just starting to turn golden. Add the thyme and remove from the heat.

Preheat your pizza oven to 500°C (932°F). Liberally dust your pizza peel with flour.

Divide the dough into four evenly sized pieces and shape each piece into a pizza about 15 cm/6 inches in diameter directly onto a lightly floured surface. Place the stretched dough bases on the pizza peel, then spread sun-dried tomato paste over two of the pizzas. Top one pizza with the aubergine slices, cherry tomatoes and half the crumbled dolcelatte cheese. Top the other pizza with pepperoni, olives and half the diced mozzarella cheese. For the third pizza, spread the pesto over the base and arrange the artichoke hearts and semi-dried tomatoes on top. Scatter the remaining mozzarella cheese over it. Garnish with basil leaves. Top the last pizza with the sautéed onions and remaining dolcelatte cheese. Season all the pizzas well.

Working quickly, slide the pizza peel into your pizza oven. Bake for 90 seconds. The crust will be golden, and the cheese melted and bubbling. Top the onion pizza with the rocket and serve immediately.

GOATS' CHEESE & PESTO PIZZETTE

The variety of goats' cheese to use here is the one with a snowy white rind that will hold its shape in the oven – just cut the pizza bases to fit the sliced cheese. Coupled with fresh pesto, this is a marriage made in heaven. The pizzette are perfect served with drinks, as they can be assembled ahead of time and cooked at the last moment. If you make them beforehand, prick the bases all over to prevent them from rising too much, add the toppings, then cover and refrigerate until ready to cook.

½ recipe Basic Pizza Dough (page 14), making just 1 ball of dough

6 tablespoons Classic Green Pesto (page 104) or store-bought fresh pesto

1 small goats' cheese log with rind (300 g/10 oz.)

4 fat garlic cloves, thinly sliced

extra virgin olive oil, to drizzle

salt and freshly ground black pepper, to season

a round cookie cutter, 7 cm/ 3 inches (optional)

a pizza peel

MAKES 12 MINI PIZZETTE, 7 CM/3 INCHES

Preheat your pizza oven to 500°C (932°F). Liberally dust your pizza peel with flour.

Uncover the dough, punch out the air and roll or pull very thinly on a well-floured surface. Using an upturned glass or a cookie cutter, stamp out twelve 7-cm/3-inch circles and lay on the floured pizza peel. Spread the pizzette with a little pesto.

Slice the goats' cheese into 12 slices and lay a slice on top of the pesto. Arrange a couple of slices of garlic on the goats' cheese and brush with olive oil. Season well. Working quickly, slide the pizza peel into your pizza oven. Bake for 90 seconds, or until the cheese is beginning to melt. Serve immediately.

LITTLE TUSCAN PIZZAS

Schiacciate ('skee-a-chah-tay') in Tuscany are individual thin, crispy pizzas with the simplest of toppings. The dough is rolled out to almost baking-parchment thinness, laid on a floured pizza peel, then topped with cheese, vegetables and prosciutto, all of which are cut wafer-thin so that they will cook quickly. Mozzarella is often used as the base instead of tomato sauce, and sliced fresh tomatoes or halved cherry tomatoes are scattered on top of the cheese. Fresh herbs or a handful of peppery rocket/arugula are often added when the pizza comes sizzling out of the oven.

1 recipe Basic Pizza Dough (page 14)

Choose from the following toppings (thinly slice any vegetables and mozzarella cheese):

salami, red onion and capers

aubergine/eggplant, red onions, fresh mozzarella cheese and fresh sage

potato, fresh mozzarella cheese, anchovy, olive and fresh sage or rosemary

courgette/zucchini, fresh mozzarella cheese, anchovy and fresh basil

fresh mozzarella cheese, tomato and rocket/arugula

extra virgin olive oil, to drizzle

salt and freshly ground black pepper, to season

a pizza peel

MAKES 6 PIZZETTE, 15 CM/
6 INCHES

Preheat your pizza oven to 500°C (932°F). Liberally dust your pizza peel with flour.

Uncover the dough, punch out the air and divide into six pieces. Shape each piece into a smooth ball and roll into a very thin circle directly onto a lightly floured surface. Put the discs on the pizza peel. Arrange a few slices of mozzarella cheese on top (if using). Toss the chosen sliced vegetables in a little olive oil and arrange sparingly on top of the pizza bases along with any other toppings.

Working quickly, slide the pizza peel into your pizza oven. Bake for 90 seconds, or until the crust is golden and crisp. Remove from the oven, scatter with any herbs, drizzle with olive oil and serve immediately.

'NDUJA & BLACK OLIVE TAPENADE PIZZETTE

The name 'tapenade' comes from the Provençal word tapena meaning 'capers' and is a thick sauce or spread made from capers, garlic and anchovies. This recipe adds rich dark olives and charred sweet (bell) pepper for a more intense, smoky flavour that is delicious with fiery 'nduja. Spread the rest on focaccia or add more oil for a dipping sauce.

½ recipe Basic Pizza Dough (page 14), making just 1 ball of dough
1 small sweet red (bell) pepper
3 garlic cloves, skins on
2–3 tablespoons salted capers
225 g/8 oz. black wrinkly olives, pitted
12 boneless anchovy fillets
about 150 ml/⅔ cup mild olive oil
freshly squeezed lemon juice, to taste
45 ml/3 tablespoons chopped fresh flat-leaf parsley
250–300 g/9–10½ oz. 'nduja (spicy Calabrian sausage)
12 cherry tomatoes, halved
extra virgin olive oil, to drizzle
fresh oregano, to garnish
salt and freshly ground black pepper, to season

a round cookie cutter, 7 cm/ 3 inches (optional)
a pizza peel

MAKES 12 MINI PIZZETTE, 7 CM/3 INCHES

Preheat your pizza oven to 500°C (932°F). Liberally dust your pizza peel with flour.

First make the tapenade. Put the whole (bell) pepper and garlic cloves under a hot grill/broiler and grill/broil for about 15 minutes, turning until completely charred all over. Cool, rub off the skin (do not wash) and remove the stalk and seeds from the pepper. Peel the skin off the garlic. Rinse the capers and drain. Put all these in a food processor with the olives and anchovies and process until roughly chopped. With the motor running, slowly add the olive oil until you have a fairly smooth dark paste (process less if you prefer it rougher). Season with lemon juice and black pepper. Stir in the parsley. Store in a jar, covered with a layer of olive oil to exclude the air, for up to 1 month.

Uncover the dough, punch out the air and roll, or pull, very thinly on a well-floured surface. Using an upturned glass or a cookie cutter, stamp out twelve 7-cm/3-inch circles and lay on the pizza peel.

Spread the pizzette with a little black olive tapenade and top with 1 heaped teaspoon of 'nduja. Push in halved cherry tomatoes then brush with olive oil. Season if necessary. Working quickly, slide the pizza peel into your pizza oven. Bake for 90 seconds. Remove from the oven, and serve immediately with oregano.

POTATO & MOZZARELLA CALZONE

In Naples, this is known as 'filled pizza' or pizza ripieno, *but the word* calzone *literally means 'trouser leg' as it was thought the shape was reminiscent of the traditional everyday dress of the street – a sort of tapered pantaloon.*

½ recipe **Basic Pizza Dough** (page 14), making just 1 ball of dough

50–75 g/2–3 oz. buffalo mozzarella cheese or cow's milk mozzarella cheese (*fior di latte*)

200 g/7 oz. potatoes, peeled, boiled and thinly sliced

2 tablespoons extra virgin olive oil, plus extra to glaze

1 garlic clove, finely chopped

1 tablespoon chopped fresh rosemary needles

salt and freshly ground black pepper, to season

a pizza peel

MAKES 1 CALZONE, 25 CM/ 10 INCHES THEN FOLDED

Preheat your pizza oven to 400°C (752°F). Liberally dust your pizza peel with flour.

Lightly squeeze any excess moisture out of the mozzarella then cut it into cubes. Toss the sliced potato with the olive oil, garlic and rosemary, then add the mozzarella cheese.

Uncover the dough, punch out the air and roll or pull into a 25-cm/10-inch circle directly onto a lightly floured surface. Slide this onto the pizza peel. Spread one half of the calzone with the potato mixture, leaving just over 1 cm/½ inch around the edge. Season well. Fold the uncovered half of the dough over the filling. Pinch and twist the edges firmly together so that the filling doesn't escape during cooking.

Working quickly, slide the pizza peel into your pizza oven. Bake for 2–3 minutes, or until the crust is puffed up and golden.

Remove from the oven and brush with a little olive oil. Leave to stand for 2–3 minutes before serving (this will allow the filling to cool slightly). Serve hot or warm.

CALZONE ALLA PARMIGIANA

This is a good calzone to make for more than two people. The vegetables can be chopped as roughly as you like, but the aubergine/eggplant must be cooked through before it goes into the dough. You can add a little Pizzaiola Sauce (page 16) to make it more tomatoey.

1 recipe Basic Pizza Dough (page 14), up to the first rising

2 roasted aubergines/ eggplants, cubed

12 roasted garlic cloves, peeled

4 tablespoons extra virgin olive oil, plus extra to drizzle

200 g/6½ oz. buffalo mozzarella or cow's milk mozzarella (*fior di latte*)

5 ripe tomatoes, cubed

3 tablespoons fresh basil, chopped

4 tablespoons freshly grated Parmesan cheese

salt and freshly ground black pepper, to season

a pizza peel

MAKES 4 CALZONE, 20 CM/ 8 INCHES THEN FOLDED

Preheat your pizza oven to 400°C (752°F). Liberally dust your pizza peel with flour.

Uncover the dough, punch out the air and divide into four balls. Dredge with flour and leave to rise on a lightly floured surface for about 20 minutes, until soft and puffy.

Lightly squeeze any excess moisture out of the mozzarella then cut it into cubes. In a large bowl, combine the roasted aubergine and garlic with the tomatoes, mozzarella and basil. Season to taste.

Roll or pull the risen balls of dough into 20-cm/8-inch circles directly onto a lightly floured surface. Place these on the pizza peel. Spread a quarter of the vegetable mixture on one half of each calzone, leaving just over 1 cm/½ inch around the edge. Season well. Fold the uncovered half of the dough over the filling. Pinch and twist the edges firmly together so that the filling doesn't escape during cooking. Brush with olive oil and sprinkle with Parmesan cheese.

Working quickly, slide the pizza peel into your pizza oven. Bake for 2–3 minutes, or until the crust is puffed up and golden. Remove from the oven and leave to stand for 2–3 minutes before serving (this will allow the filling to cool slightly). Serve hot or warm.

PIZZA RUSTICA

Italians are very thrifty, and a really delicious double-crust pizza can be made with a carefully chosen mixture of leftovers. There must be cheese or béchamel sauce to keep it moist, but you can add anchovies, cooked meat sauce, capers, olives – whatever you like, as long as their flavours suit each other.

15 g/½ oz. fresh/compressed yeast

a pinch of caster/granulated sugar

250 ml/1 cup warm water

350 g/2⅓ cups plain white/all-purpose flour, plus extra to dust

1 tablespoon olive oil, plus extra for brushing

a pinch of salt

FILLING

100 g/3½ oz. cubed fresh mozzarella

100 g/3½ oz. cubed salami, ham or cooked sausage

50 g/⅓ cup cooked chopped spinach

4 sun-dried tomatoes in oil, chopped

3–4 tablespoons tomato sauce, Salsa Pizzaiola (page 16) or similar

2–3 tablespoons chopped mixed fresh herbs

salt and freshly ground black pepper, to season

a pizza peel

MAKES 2

To make the dough, put the fresh yeast and sugar in a medium bowl and beat until creamy. Whisk in the warm water and leave for 10 minutes until frothy. Sift the flour into a large bowl and make a hollow in the centre. Pour in the yeast mixture, olive oil and a good pinch of salt. Mix with a round-bladed knife, then your hands, until the dough comes together. Transfer to a floured surface, wash and dry your hands and knead for 10 minutes until smooth and elastic. Put the dough in a clean, oiled bowl, cover wrap and let rise until doubled in size – about 1 hour.

Preheat your pizza oven to 400°C (752°F). Liberally dust your pizza peel with flour.

To make the filling, put the mozzarella, salami, spinach, sun-dried tomatoes, tomato sauce and mixed herbs in a bowl and season with salt and pepper.

Roll out the dough to a large circle, making sure it is well floured so it doesn't stick. Place the stretched dough base on the pizza peel. Pile the filling onto one half of the dough, avoiding the edges. Flip over the other half to cover, press the edges together to seal, then twist and crimp. Brush lightly with olive oil. Make a slash in the top or it could explode when cooking.

Working quickly, slide the pizza peel into your pizza oven. Bake for 2–3 minutes, or until the crust is golden and firm. Remove from the oven, set aside for 5 minutes, then serve.

4

FOCACCIA

SIMPLE THIN FOCACCIA

This is a wonderful example of the traditional focaccia, as it is baked directly on the pizza peel. It's a classic recipe that is perfect for sharing over drinks or as an appetizer. This is the kind of focaccia that you tear and dip into yet more fruity olive oil, either on your own or accompanied by friends and family.

½ recipe Basic Focaccia **Dough (page 18), risen once but uncooked**
50 ml/¼ cup extra virgin olive oil
sea salt flakes

a pizza peel

SERVES 3–4

Uncover the risen dough, punch out the air and divide into two. Shape each piece into a rough ball then pull and stretch the dough to a large oval shape – as large as will fit on the peel. Place on the pizza peel. Cover and leave to rise for approximately 30 minutes.

Preheat your pizza oven to 350°C (662°F). Liberally dust your pizza peel with flour.

Uncover and, using your fingertips, make deep dimples all over the surface of the dough right down to the peel. Drizzle over all but 1 tablespoons of the remaining olive oil. Spray the focaccia with water and sprinkle generously with salt flakes.

Working quickly, slide the pizza peel into your pizza oven. Bake for 4–5 minutes, or until the crust is golden. Brush or drizzle with the remaining olive oil then transfer to a wire rack to cool before eating. Serve with a small bowl of extra virgin olive oil for dipping.

ROAST GARLIC ROSEMARY FOCACCIA

Freshly made focaccia is always a treat, with roast garlic adding a wonderful savouriness and rosemary an appealing aromatic note. Serve on its own or with Italian charcuterie, such as Parma ham/ prosciutto or mortadella, for a light meal.

500 g/3½ cups strong white bread flour, plus extra for dusting

1 teaspoon fast-action/quick rising dried yeast

1 teaspoon fine sea salt

1 teaspoon caster/granulated sugar

300 ml/1¼ cups hand-hot water

5 tablespoons extra virgin olive oil

6 roast garlic cloves, peeled and chopped

3 tablespoons rosemary needles, finely chopped

sea salt flakes

a pizza peel

SERVES 6

Mix together the flour, yeast, salt and sugar. Gradually add in the water and 2 tablespoons of the oil, bringing the mixture together to form a sticky dough. Turn out onto a lightly floured surface and knead until smooth and elastic. Then work in the roast garlic and 2 tablespoons of the rosemary. Transfer the dough to an oiled mixing bowl, cover and set aside in a warm place to rise for 1 hour. Liberally dust your pizza peel with flour.

Break down the risen dough and shape into a large oval on the pizza peel.

Using your fingertips, press into the dough to make numerous small indentations. Spoon over 2 tablespoons of the oil, so that it fills the indents, and sprinkle over the remaining rosemary. Set aside to rest for 30 minutes.

Preheat your pizza oven to 350°C (662°F).

Working quickly, slide the peel into your pizza peel. Bake for 4–5 minutes, or until golden brown. Spoon over the remaining oil and sprinkle with the sea salt flakes. Serve warm from the oven or at room temperature.

FENNEL & TOMATO FOCACCIA

Fennel is widely eaten in Italy, and often served in a salad, finely shaved and simply dressed with olive oil, lemon juice and black pepper. Here its aniseedy flavour is enhanced with roasting and, along with the tomatoes, makes a substantial topping for a simple focaccia dough.

1 recipe Basic Focaccia Dough (page 18), risen once and uncooked
2 baby fennel bulbs, thinly sliced and fronds chopped
2 tomatoes, thinly sliced
1½ teaspoons sea salt flakes
extra virgin olive oil, to serve

a flame-proof, cast-iron skillet or griddle pan, oiled

SERVES 6–8

Uncover the risen dough and put it onto a lightly floured surface. Using a lightly floured rolling pin, gently roll from the centre upwards in one motion, not pressing too firmly so that any air bubbles stay intact. Roll from the centre down to the opposite end and shape to fit into the pan. Place into the prepared pan. Lightly cover and let sit again for 20–30 minutes until it has risen.

Preheat your pizza oven to 350°C (662°F).

Use the tips of your fingers to press dimples over the surface of the dough. Lay the fennel and tomato slices on top and scatter with the fronds. Drizzle with the remaining olive oil and sprinkle with the salt flakes. Working quickly, slide the pan into your pizza oven. Bake for 4–5 minutes, or until the crust is golden. Remove from the oven and let cool before eating.

Serve with a small bowl of extra virgin olive oil for dipping.

SARDENAIRA

This large savoury Ligurian focaccia is topped with salted anchovies or salted sardines (hence the name). It is perfect for outdoor eating, served in thin slices with a cold glass of wine or beer.

25 g/1 cake fresh/compressed yeast, 1 tablespoon dried active baking yeast or 2 teaspoons fast-action/quick rising dried yeast

½ teaspoon caster/granulated sugar

150 ml/⅔ cup warm milk

500 g/4¼ cups Italian '00' flour

7 tablespoons extra virgin olive oil

6 tablespoons hand-hot water

2 onions, thinly sliced

1 kg/2¼ lb. fresh, very ripe tomatoes, peeled and chopped

100 g/3½ oz. anchovies or sardines in salt

12 or more whole garlic cloves, unpeeled

100 g/3½ oz. or more small pitted black olives (ideally Ligurian)

1 tablespoon dried oregano

salt and freshly ground black pepper, to season

a flame-proof, cast-iron skillet or griddle pan, oiled

SERVES 10

In a large bowl, cream the fresh yeast with the sugar and whisk in the warm milk. Leave for 10 minutes until frothy. For other yeasts, follow the manufacturer's instructions.

Sift the flour with 1 teaspoon of salt into a large bowl and make a well in the centre. Pour in the yeast mixture, 4 tablespoons of the olive oil and the hand-hot water. Mix together with a round-bladed knife, then use your hands until the dough comes together. Tip out onto a lightly floured surface, wash and dry your hands, then knead briskly for 10–15 minutes until smooth, shiny and elastic. Try not to add any extra flour at this stage – a wetter dough is better. If necessary, flour your hands and not the dough. If it is really too soft to handle, knead in a little more flour.

To test if the dough is ready, roll it into a fat sausage, take each end in either hand, lift the dough up and pull and stretch it outwards, gently wiggling it up and down – it should stretch out quite easily. If it doesn't, it needs more kneading. Shape into a neat ball. Put it in an oiled bowl, cover and leave to rise in a warm, draught-free place until doubled in size – about 1½ hours.

Heat the remaining olive oil in a large pan, add the onions and cook for 10 minutes or until softened and lightly coloured. Add the tomatoes and cook gently until collapsed and very thick. Split the anchovies, remove the backbone, rinse and roughly chop. Stir into the sauce and season to taste.

Preheat your pizza oven to 350°C (662°F).

Knock back the dough, knead lightly, then stretch and pat it out into the prepared pan, pushing the dough well up the edges. Spread the sauce on top of the dough, cover with the whole garlic cloves and the olives, then sprinkle with the oregano. Drizzle with a little olive oil and bake for 4–5 minutes, until golden. Serve sliced – hot, warm or cold.

RUSTIC FOCACCIA
WITH RED PEPPER & ONION

Light and simple, this flavoursome focaccia is great served to accompany soup and makes a tasty addition to any picnic basket.

½ recipe Basic Focaccia
Dough (page 18), making
just 1 focaccia, with
1 teaspoon dried basil
added to the flour

TOPPING

3½ tablespoons extra virgin
olive oil

½ red (bell) pepper, deseeded
and thinly sliced

½ red onion, thinly sliced

*a flame-proof, cast-iron skillet
or griddle pan, oiled*

SERVES 4–6

Make the Basic Focaccia Dough following the recipe on page 18, adding 1 teaspoon dried basil to the flour and leaving out the rosemary. Knead the dough, transfer to an oiled bowl, and give it the first rising.

Uncover the mixing bowl and transfer the ball of dough to a well-floured surface. Knead well for a couple of minutes, then leave to rest for 5 minutes.

Roll out the dough with a rolling pin until big enough to fit your pan. Transfer to the prepared pan. Push your finger into the dough repeatedly to make dents about 2 cm/1 inch apart all over the surface.

For the topping, drizzle the oil evenly over the focaccia and scatter the pepper and onion over the top. Cover and leave to rest for another 40 minutes. It will increase in size again.

Preheat your pizza oven to 350°C (662°F).

Uncover the focaccia and cook for 4–5 minutes. Once cooked, remove from the oven and let it cool before eating.

FOCACCIA ALLA DIAVOLA

This is a good, fiery focaccia for making sandwiches or serving in thick slices smothered in fresh ricotta. Replacing some of the liquid in the dough with tomato purée/paste (or even all the water with tomato juice) gives it a beautiful, rusty red colour, studded with bright red pepper and dark chunks of salami or chorizo.

½ recipe Basic Focaccia Dough (page 18), making the changes stated in this recipe

4 tablespoons tomato purée/paste

4–6 red chillies/chiles or Peppadews, diced

2 red (bell) peppers, roasted, deseeded and diced

100 g/3½ oz. *salame piccante* or chorizo, cubed

75 g/2½ oz. *provolone piccante*, Emmental or Gruyère cheese, cubed

100 ml/⅓ cup extra virgin olive oil, plus extra to drizzle

sea salt flakes

a flame-proof, cast-iron skillet or griddle pan, oiled

SERVES 3–4

Make the focaccia dough following the recipe on page 18, but using 4 tablespoons tomato purée dissolved in the water. Knead the dough and give it the first rising.

Uncover the dough, punch out the air and pull or roll it out into a rough circle. Dot with the chillies, red peppers, salami, provolone and lots of freshly ground black pepper. Flip one half of the dough over and lightly knead to incorporate the ingredients. Shape into a rough ball on a lightly floured surface and pat into the prepared pan. Cover and leave to rise for 30 minutes.

Uncover and, using your fingertips, make deep dimples all over the surface of the dough. Drizzle over the olive oil, re-cover very lightly with clingfilm and leave to rise for a final 30 minutes until very puffy.

Preheat your pizza oven to 350°C (662°F).

Uncover the focaccia, mist with water and sprinkle generously with salt flakes. Working quickly, slide the pan into your pizza oven. Bake for 4–5 minutes, until risen and golden. Transfer to a wire rack, brush with olive oil and leave to cool before eating.

POTATO & OLIVE FOCACCIA

Making a bread by mixing mashed potato with flour and anointing it lavishly with good olive oil is common all over Italy, especially in Liguria and Puglia, where some of the best olive oil comes from.

450 g/1 lb. baking potatoes, unpeeled

625 g/5¼ cups Italian '00' flour

½ teaspoon fine sea salt

25 g/1 cake fresh/compressed yeast, 1 packet active dried baking yeast, or 2 teaspoons fast-active/quick rising dried yeast

180 g/6½ oz. large, juicy green olives, pits in

150 ml/⅔ cup extra virgin olive oil

sea salt flakes

a flame-proof, cast-iron skillet or griddle pan, oiled

SERVES 4–6

Boil or bake the potatoes in their skins and peel them whilst still warm. Mash them or pass them through a potato ricer.

Sift the flour with the fine salt into a large bowl and make a well in the centre. Crumble in the fresh yeast, or add dried yeast, if using. If you are using dried yeast, follow the manufacturer's instructions. Add the potatoes and mix together with your hands until the dough comes together. Tip out onto a floured surface, wash and dry your hands and knead energetically for 10 minutes until smooth and elastic. The dough should be soft; if it isn't, add a couple of tablespoons warm water.

Divide the dough into two, shape each piece into a round ball on a lightly floured surface and roll out into two circles or one large rectangle to fit whichever pan you are using. Put the dough in the pan, cover and leave to rise for 2 hours.

Uncover the dough, scatter over the olives, and, using your fingertips, make deep dimples all over the surface of the dough, pushing in some of the olives here and there. Drizzle with two-thirds of the olive oil, re-cover and leave to rise for another 30 minutes.

Preheat your pizza oven to 350°C (662°F).

Uncover the dough, spray with water and sprinkle generously with salt flakes. Working quickly, slide the pan into your pizza oven. Bake for 4–5 minutes, until risen and golden brown. Brush or drizzle with the remaining olive oil then transfer to a wire rack to cool before eating.

BLACK GRAPE SCHIACCIATA

This is a delicious bread to serve warm from the oven at breakfast time. This recipe uses fresh black grapes, but it can also be made successfully using semi-dried Montepulciano grapes. If you wanted to try something similar, you could substitute semi-dried cherries or plump Lexia raisins.

80 ml/⅓ cup extra virgin olive oil

a handful of fresh rosemary needles

450 g/3½ cups strong white bread flour

1 teaspoon fine sea salt

2 tablespoons caster/granulated sugar

1 teaspoon fast-action/quick rising dried yeast

250 ml/1 cup hand-hot water

400 g/14 oz. seedless black grapes

a flame-proof, cast-iron skillet or griddle pan, oiled

SERVES 4–6

Put the olive oil and rosemary in a bowl. Give the rosemary several good squeezes to release the aroma into the oil. Set aside for a few minutes.

Put the flour, salt and 1 tablespoon of the sugar in a large bowl and stir well. Add the yeast and stir again. Pour in 2 tablespoons of the infused, strained olive oil and enough hand-hot water to make a soft but not sticky dough.

Turn the dough out on to a lightly floured work surface and knead for 5 minutes, until the dough is smooth and elastic. Fold in the grapes and knead for a further 2–3 minutes. The dough may become sticky at this point, so dust with a little extra flour if necessary.

Press the dough into the prepared baking pan and push it with your knuckles to fill the pan. Leave to rise in a warm place for about 40 minutes, or until it has doubled in size.

Preheat your pizza oven to 350°C (662°F).

Drizzle the remaining infused olive oil over the risen dough and scatter some of the rosemary needles and the remaining sugar evenly across the top. Working quickly, slide the pan into your pizza oven. Bake for 4–5 minutes, or until the surface is golden brown and the base sounds hollow when tapped. Cool on a wire rack before eating.

CRISPY OLIVE SCHIACCIATE

Schiacciata is a dialect word meaning 'flattened', so pizza is sometimes known as schiacciata, i.e. a flattened bread dough. If, after making pizza, you find you have some dough left over (and some good olives to hand) this is the recipe for you. No olive oil is needed here, but you can have some really good oil in a little pot ready for dipping the hot pizzas into.

any leftover Basic Pizza Dough (page 14)

a splash of white wine

a handful of green olives, pitted and roughly chopped

sea salt flakes

extra virgin olive oil or Black Olive & Tomato Relish (page 107), to serve

a pizza peel

SERVES 4–6

Preheat your pizza oven to 350°C (662°F). Liberally dust your pizza peel with flour.

Using a rolling pin, roll the dough out as thinly as you can, directly onto a lightly floured surface. Place the stretched dough base on the pizza peel. Brush the dough with a little white wine, scatter with the olives and sprinkle with salt flakes. Lightly press the olives and salt into the dough. Using a pizza wheel, score the dough in diamond shapes directly on the baking sheet.

Working quickly, slide the pizza peel into your pizza oven. Bake for 1–2 minutes, until the schiacciate are puffed and pale golden. Remove from the oven and break up into the pre-cut diamonds.

Serve warm with extra virgin olive oil or Black Olive & Tomato Relish for dipping.

CHERRY TOMATO & OLIVE FOCACCIA

Homemade focaccia, served warm from the oven, is a real treat. This colourful loaf, studded with red cherry tomatoes and black olives, makes a great mealtime centrepiece, accompanied by cheeses and charcuterie.

500 g/4 cups strong white bread flour

1 teaspoon fast acting/quick rising dried yeast

1 teaspoon fine sea salt

1 teaspoon sugar

300 ml/1¼ cups hand-hot water

5 tablespoons extra virgin olive oil

12 cherry tomatoes, halved

12 black olives, pitted

a few sprigs of fresh thyme

a pinch of sea salt flakes, to serve

a pizza peel

SERVES 6

Mix together the flour, yeast, salt and sugar. Gradually add in the water and 2 tablespoons of the oil, bringing the mixture together to form a sticky dough. Turn out onto a lightly floured surface and knead until smooth and elastic. Transfer to the prepared mixing bowl, cover and set aside in a warm place to rise for 1 hour. Liberally dust your pizza peel with flour.

Break down the risen dough and shape into a large oval on the prepared pizza peel.

Using your fingers, press into the dough forming numerous small indents in it. Fill the indents with the tomatoes and olives and spoon over 2 tablespoons of the oil so that it fills any empty indents. Sprinkle with thyme and set aside to rest for 30 minutes.

Preheat your pizza oven to 350°C (662°F).

Bake the focaccia in the preheated oven for 4–5 minutes, until golden-brown. Spoon over the remaining tablespoon of oil and sprinkle with salt flakes.

Serve warm from the oven or at room temperature.

5

SAUCES
& SIDES

CHILLI/CHILE OIL opposite, left

A great addition to any pizza maker's store cupboard. Once strained the oil will keep in the fridge for a month but return to room temperature before use.

30 g/6 whole dried chillies/ chiles
250 ml/1 cup peanut oil

a sterilized glass bottle with an airtight cap

MAKES 250 ML/1 CUP

Put the chillies in a bowl, cover with hot water and leave to soak for 30 minutes until slightly softened. Drain well and discard the water. Put the softened chillies in a food processor and blend to a rough paste.

Transfer the paste to a small saucepan, pour in the oil and set over a medium heat to warm gently, until the mixtures comes to the boil. Boil for 1 minute then remove the pan from the heat and leave to cool completely.

Strain the oil through a fine mesh sieve/strainer, pour into a sterilized glass bottle and seal. Keep in the fridge for up to a month and use as required.

GARLIC OIL opposite, right

This oil is particularly good as a drizzle or dip but as it doesn't keep as well as chilli/chile oil, store in the fridge.

1 whole bulb garlic
125 ml/½ cup peanut oil

a sterilized glass bottle with an airtight cap

MAKES 125 ML/½ CUP

Peel each garlic clove and cut into 3 mm/⅛ inch slices.

Put the peanut oil in a small saucepan and set over a low heat until shimmering. Add the garlic slices and cook for about 20 minutes until they are crisp and golden but not burnt.

Remove the garlic with a slotted spoon and drain on kitchen paper/paper towels. Reserve the oil, straining several times through a fine mesh sieve/strainer to discard any small bits of garlic and set aside to cool completely. Pour into a sterilized glass bottle and seal. Keep in the fridge for up to 2 weeks and use as required.

CLASSIC GREEN PESTO

Don't stint on the fresh basil here – it is instrumental in making this the most wonderful sauce in the world! Adding a little softened butter at the end gives the pesto a creaminess. The texture is ideal when the pesto is pounded by hand, so try it once and you'll never make it in a food processor again! Pesto can be frozen successfully – some suggest leaving out the cheese and beating it in when the pesto has thawed, but it can also be included in the beginning.

2 garlic cloves
50 g/½ cup pine nuts
50 g/2 handfuls fresh basil
  leaves
150 ml/⅔ cup extra virgin
  olive oil, plus extra
  to preserve
50 g/3 tablespoons unsalted
  butter, softened
4 tablespoons/¼ cup freshly
  grated Parmesan cheese
salt and freshly ground
  black pepper, to season

MAKES ABOUT 250 ML/1 CUP

Peel the garlic and put it in a pestle and mortar with a little salt and the pine nuts. Pound until broken up (A). Add the basil leaves, a few at a time, pounding and mixing to a paste (B). Gradually beat in the olive oil, little by little, until the mixture is creamy and thick (C).

Alternatively, put everything in a food processor and process until just smooth.

Beat in the butter and season with pepper, then beat in the Parmesan cheese (D).

Spoon into a sterilized screw-top jar with a layer of olive oil on top to exclude the air, then keep in fridge for up to 2 weeks, until needed.

(See also image on page 106, top right.)

A

B

C

D

FIERY RED PESTO

opposite, bottom right

With rich sun-dried tomatoes, earthy red (bell) pepper and just a hint of chilli/chile powder, this is a delicious variation on green pesto.

1 large red (bell) pepper
2 handfuls fresh basil leaves
1 garlic clove
30 g/⅓ cup toasted pine nuts
6 sun-dried tomatoes in oil, drained and chopped
2 ripe tomatoes, skinned
3 tablespoons tomato purée/paste
½ teaspoon chilli/chili powder
50 g/½ cup freshly grated Parmesan cheese
150 ml/⅔ cup olive oil, plus extra to preserve

MAKES ABOUT 350 ML/1½ CUPS

Preheat the grill/broiler to high.

Place the pepper on the grill rack and grill/broil, turning occasionally, until charred all over. Put the pepper in a covered bowl until cool enough to handle, then peel off the skin. Halve and remove the core and seeds.

Place the pepper and the remaining ingredients, except the oil, in a food processor. Process until smooth, then, with the machine running, slowly add the oil.

Spoon the pesto into a sterilized screw-top jar with a layer of olive oil on top to exclude the air, then store in the fridge for up to two weeks, until needed.

BLACK OLIVE & TOMATO RELISH

opposite, left

This can be used as a pizza base sauce or to spread on foccacias and other breads. It's easy to make and full of rich Italian flavours.

2 tablespoons sun-dried tomato oil
1 red onion, peeled and diced
1 garlic clove, peeled and crushed
5 plump sun-dried tomatoes in oil, drained and diced
250 g/8 oz. black olives, pitted
1 bay leaf
15 fresh basil leaves, torn into pieces
freshly squeezed juice of 1 lemon
3–4 tablespoons extra virgin olive oil, plus extra to preserve
salt and freshly ground black pepper, to season

MAKES ABOUT 350 ML/1½ CUPS

In a medium saucepan, heat the sun-dried tomato oil and gently sweat the onion and garlic for a few minutes. Add the sun-dried tomatoes, olives and bay leaf and continue to cook for a few minutes until the flavours have melded.

Season, remove from the heat and discard the bay leaf. Pour the mixture into a food processor with the basil and process to a coarse purée. Add the lemon juice and oil. Season, if needed.

Spoon the relish into a sterilized screw-top jar with a layer of olive oil to exclude the air, then store in the fridge for up to two weeks, until needed.

SUN-BLUSH TOMATO PESTO

Sun-blush tomatoes are a hybrid between sun-dried and oven-roasted. More subtle in taste, they are softer and juicier than sun-dried.

150 g/5½ oz. sun-blush tomatoes, drained

100 g/3½ oz. pine nuts, toasted

1 garlic clove

60 g/2 oz. freshly grated Parmesan cheese

1 teaspoon crushed dried chilli/hot red pepper flakes

125 ml/½ cup extra virgin olive oil

salt and freshly ground black pepper, to season

MAKES 500 ML/2 CUPS

In a food processor, combine the tomatoes, pine nuts, garlic, Parmesan cheese and chilli flakes. Keep the motor running and slowly pour in the olive oil. Add salt and pepper to taste.

Spoon the pesto into an airtight container. Once sealed, it will keep in the fridge for up to 1 week.

ROASTED TOMATOES

These are wonderful in just about any recipe, from pasta to pizza.

6 large Italian plum tomatoes

2 garlic cloves, thickly sliced

1 teaspoon salt

½ teaspoon freshly ground black pepper

2 tablespoons olive oil

1 tablespoon balsamic vinegar

MAKES 12 HALVES

Preheat a conventional oven to 170°C (325°F) Gas 3.

Slice the tomatoes in half lengthways. Place in a large roasting tin lined with foil. Sprinkle the garlic, salt and pepper over and drizzle with olive oil. Bake in the preheated oven for 45 minutes. Remove, drizzle with vinegar and let sit for 10 minutes.

When cool, pack into an airtight container. Once sealed, the tomatoes will keep in the fridge for up to 1 week.

ROASTED FENNEL

Liquorice-flavoured fennel becomes very sweet when roasted. A little boiling water in the tin keeps the flesh soft while the edges crisp up and caramelize.

4 large fennel bulbs
2 garlic cloves, thickly sliced
1 teaspoon salt
½ teaspoon freshly ground black pepper
2 tablespoons olive oil
1 tablespoon balsamic vinegar

MAKES 8–10 SLICES

Preheat a conventional oven to 170°C (325°F) Gas 3.

Cut the fennel in half lengthways and cut the core out. Slice the pieces about 1.5 cm/½ inch thick and place in a large roasting tin lined with aluminium foil. Sprinkle the garlic, salt and pepper over and drizzle with olive oil. Put the fennel in the preheated oven to roast for 1 hour. About 15 minutes into the cooking time pour 125 ml/½ cup of boiling water into the tin. When cooked, drizzle with the vinegar.

Once cool, pack in an airtight container. Once sealed the fennel will keep in the fridge for up to 1 week.

CARAMELIZED ONIONS

You can buy jars of caramelized onion jam but homemade are much tastier.

3 tablespoons olive oil
2 large onions, sliced thinly
1 tablespoon red wine vinegar
1 teaspoon caster/granulated sugar
1 teaspoon fine sea salt
½ teaspoon freshly ground
   black pepper

MAKES 350 G/1½ CUPS

Heat the oil in a large frying pan/skillet. Add the onions, salt and pepper and fry for three minutes over a high heat. Turn the heat down to medium/low and fry for 20 minutes more.

Add the vinegar and sugar and cook for 5 more minutes. Remove from the heat. When cool, spoon into an airtight container. Refrigerate for up to 1 week.

GIARDINIERA

Do try these delicious little pickles.

½ small head of cauliflower
1 red (bell) pepper, cored and
   deseeded
2 medium carrots
2 celery sticks, sliced
40 g/½ cup Sicilian green olives,
   pitted
30 g/¼ cup peperoncini (pickled
   hot peppers)

PICKLING LIQUID
300 ml/1¼ cups white wine
   vinegar
350 ml/1½ cups water
75 g/⅓ cup caster/granulated
   sugar
2½ tablespoons fine sea salt
a pinch of dried chilli/hot red
   pepper flakes
½ teaspoon yellow mustard seeds

MAKES 400 G/3 CUPS

Chop all of the vegetables into 1.5-cm/½-inch pieces.

Pour the pickling liquid ingredients into a saucepan and heat until the sugar is dissolved. Let cool.

Bring a large saucepan of salted water to the boil. Blanch all the vegetables (except for the olives and peperoncini) individually. Refresh them in a bowl of iced water and drain on kitchen paper/paper towels. Add to the pickling liquid. Weight the pickles down with a plate to keep them submerged and put in fridge, covered, for 24 hours before using.

The pickles will keep in the fridge for up to 2 weeks.

GARDEN HERB BUTTER

This is a wonderful green butter that just says it all. Fresh from the garden or farmers' market, make sure you use freshly picked herbs. Don't freeze this butter as the herbs tend to go black and lose their flavour. Spread it on breads or scones and dollop on top of roasted vegetables to add a whole new spin.

1 stick/120 g unsalted butter, at room temperature

2 generous tablespoons fresh oregano leaves

2 generous tablespoons fresh marjoram leaves

2 generous tablespoons fresh thyme leaves

1 generous tablespoon fresh rosemary needles

salt and freshly ground black pepper

MAKES GENEROUS 130 G/ ½ CUP

Put all the ingredients in a food processor and process until smooth but leaving a little texture in the butter. Refrigerate until ready to use.

To make a butter roll, spoon the butter mixture onto a piece of plastic wrap/clingfilm. Fold the wrap/film over the butter and roll into a sausage shape. Twist the ends to secure and store in the fridge. When you're ready to use the butter, slice off discs as desired.

To use, melt over grilled vegetables or spread on breads.

MAYOS

Homemade mayonnaise is far more tasty than store-bought versions and using a food processor means it's so simple to make.

CLASSIC MAYO

3 egg yolks
2 teaspoons Dijon
  mustard
2 teaspoons white wine
  vinegar or freshly
  squeezed lemon juice

½ teaspoon sea salt
300 ml/1¼ cups olive oil

MAKES ABOUT 400 ML/
1¾ CUPS

Put the egg yolks, mustard, vinegar or lemon juice and salt in a food processor and blend until foaming. With the blade running, gradually pour in the oil through a funnel until thick and glossy. If it is too thick add a little water. Taste and adjust the seasoning, if necessary.

Spoon into a bowl and serve. Keep in the fridge for up to 3 days in an airtight container.

MUSTARD MAYO

1 recipe Classic Mayo
2 tablespoons wholegrain mustard

MAKES ABOUT 400 ML/1¾ CUPS

Make the Classic Mayo following the method in the recipe, left, but omitting the Dijon mustard. Transfer to a bowl and stir in the wholegrain mustard. Use as required or store as before.

HERB MAYO

1 recipe Classic Mayo
a handful of any fresh green herbs, such as basil, parsley or tarragon, chopped

MAKES ABOUT 400 ML/1¾ CUPS

Make the Classic Mayo following the method in the recipe, far left. Add the herbs to the food processor and blend until the sauce is speckled green. Use as required or store as before.

LEMON MAYO

1 recipe Classic Mayo
1 teaspoon freshly squeezed lemon juice
1 teaspoon finely grated lemon zest
a pinch of freshly ground black pepper

MAKES ABOUT 400 ML/1¾ CUPS

Make the Classic Mayo following the method in the recipe, far left, adding the lemon juice, zest and pepper with the mustard and vinegar. Blend until thickened. Use as required or store as before.

Variation: For a Lime Mayo, simply replace the lemon zest and juice with the zest and juice from a lime.

PESTO MAYO

1 recipe Classic Mayo
1 teaspoon Classic Green Pesto (page 104) or store-bought fresh pesto

MAKES ABOUT 400 ML/1¾ CUPS

Make the Classic Mayo following the method in the recipe, far left, adding the pesto at the same time as the mustard and vinegar. Blend until thickened. Use as required or store as before.

BLACK OLIVES SOTT'OLIO

*Both of these olive recipes will keep well in a cool, dark place for weeks
– or even months, if they get the chance. Sott'olio means 'under oil'.*

**4 tablespoons coriander
seeds, crushed**

**2 tablespoons black
peppercorns**

**8 garlic cloves, halved
lengthways**

**750 g/5 cups black olives
in brine, drained, patted
dry and pricked with a fork
or sharp knife**

**zest of 1 large, unwaxed
lemon, removed in long
strips**

**750 ml/3 cups extra virgin
olive oil**

*1.5 litre/6 cups or 3 x 500 ml/
1 pint jars, sterilized*

**MAKES 1 LARGE OR 3 SMALL
JARS**

Put the coriander seeds, peppercorns and garlic into a dry frying
pan/skillet and cook over a gentle heat, shaking and toasting until
aromatic: do not let them scorch. Stir in the olives and cook for
2–3 minutes. Put the still-hot, sterilized jars onto a folded cloth
or wooden board. Using a sterilized spoon, transfer the mixture
into the jar(s). Push the lemon zest into the jar(s) using sterilized
metal tongs.

Put the oil into a saucepan and heat until a small cube of bread
turns golden brown in 40 seconds. Let cool for 2 minutes, then
pour the oil carefully into the jar(s) until covered. Let cool,
uncovered and undisturbed. Top up with any unused oil, cover
and seal tightly. Store in a cool, dark cupboard until ready
to serve.

GREEN OLIVES WITH FENNEL

If you have fennel flowers in your garden, use the whole seed heads for this dish. Otherwise, use fennel seeds.

500 g/3 cups preserved green olives, washed and dried with kitchen paper, then pricked with a fork

500 ml/2 cups extra virgin olive oil

2 whole bulbs of fresh garlic, halved crossways

4–8 fresh fennel flower heads, seeds intact (optional)

3 tablespoons black peppercorns, cracked or coarsely crushed

2 tablespoons fennel seeds

1 teaspoon cloves

1 litre/4 cups or 2 x 500 ml/ 1 pint jars, sterilized

MAKES 1 LARGE OR 2 MEDIUM JARS

Pack the olives loosely into the jar(s) with tongs or a spoon, but not your fingers.

Put the oil into a heavy-based saucepan and heat until a small cube of bread turns golden brown in about 40 seconds. Using a slotted spoon, lower the halved garlic bulbs and the fennel flower heads into the oil. Let them sizzle briefly, for about 30 seconds, then lift them out and divide evenly between the jar(s). Scatter in the peppercorns, fennel seeds and cloves. Top up with the remaining olives.

Pour the sizzling hot oil carefully over the olives until covered. Let cool for about 2 minutes, then pour the remaining oil carefully into the jar(s) until completely filled. Let cool, uncovered and undisturbed. Seal tightly and store in a cool, dark cupboard until ready to serve.

TOMATO, MOZZARELLA & BASIL SALAD

Insalata Caprese, the classic salad born on the Isle of Capri, is hard to beat. It combines three ingredients that work in total harmony with each other. The first is mozzarella, preferably soft, creamy mozzarella di bufala; then tomato – this must be red and ripe, and the same size as the ball of mozzarella – and basil, which must be fresh, pungent and plentiful. Although not strictly Italian, sliced avocado is a delicious addition. To make this salad really sing of sunny Italy, use the best possible ingredients and be generous with them.

2 balls of buffalo mozzarella cheese or cow's milk mozzarella cheese (*fior de latte*), 150-g/5-oz.

2 large ripe tomatoes, roughly the same size as the balls of mozzarella

50 g/2 oz. fresh basil leaves

about 100 ml/½ cup extra virgin olive oil

salt and freshly ground black pepper, to season

SERVES 4

Cut the mozzarella and tomatoes into slices about 5 mm/¼ inch thick. Arrange the tomato slices on a large plate and season with salt and pepper. Put a slice of mozzarella on each slice of tomato and top with a basil leaf. Tear up the remaining basil and scatter over the top. Drizzle with a generous amount of olive oil just before serving.

This salad must be made at the last moment to prevent the tomatoes from weeping and the mozzarella from drying out. Serve at room temperature, never chilled, as this would kill the flavours.

Variation: If using avocado, halve and peel a ripe avocado, remove the stone and slice the flesh. Intersperse the slices of avocado with the tomato and mozzarella.

TOMATO & MINT SALAD

The taste of the salad reflects the Sicilian region's Byzantine flavour, typified by the mint, which releases a special flavour when blended with red onions. Be discerning when choosing tomatoes. Cherry tomatoes on the vine have a reliably good flavour compared to other varieties. Buy them when they're firm and bright in colour. In Italy, Spain and France you can buy your tomatoes in so many different degrees of ripeness. You will often be asked if you want to eat them that day, the next day or use them to make a sauce. It can be an enjoyable experience being allowed to choose the different tomatoes. To pick the best ones, smell the stalk end – they should smell peppery.

4 firm, bright red tomatoes
½ a small red onion
a handful of fresh mint leaves
2 tablespoons extra virgin olive oil
1 tablespoon balsamic vinegar
25 g/1 oz. freshly grated Parmesan cheese shavings
salt and freshly ground black pepper, to season
crusty or French bread, to serve

SERVES 4

Cut the tomatoes into slices and slice the onion into rings. Roughly chop the mint.

Arrange the tomatoes and onions on a serving plate before adding the mint. Season to taste, then pour over the extra virgin olive oil and balsamic vinegar.

Sprinkle over the Parmesan cheese shavings and serve with bread.

INSALATA DI CAMPO

*In Italian markets, you see small boxes of different baby leaves, often wild. Shoppers choose a handful each of their favourite kinds to make a mixed salad. Originally, the mixture was picked from wild plants in the fields (*campo *means 'field') and still is in country areas, so the mixture should include herbs, bitter leaves, soft greens and crunchy leaves.*

350 g/¾ lb. wild salad leaves or herbs

1 tablespoon balsamic vinegar

6–8 tablespoons extra virgin olive oil

freshly squeezed juice of ½ a lemon

salt and freshly ground black pepper, to season

50 g/2 oz. hard cheese, such as Parmesan, to serve

SERVES 4–6

Wash the leaves well in a large bowl of cold water. Drain and shake or spin them dry without crushing or bruising them. Transfer to a clean cloth lined with kitchen paper/paper towels, wrap in the cloth and keep in the fridge for about 30 minutes.

Put the vinegar, oil, lemon juice, salt and pepper into a bowl and whisk well to form a dressing.

Using a swivel-bladed vegetable peeler, remove fine, long, thin curls of cheese from the block, then set them aside.

When ready to serve, put the leaves into a salad bowl. Whisk the dressing briefly and sprinkle over the salad. Toss gently until everything gleams, then top with the cheese shavings and serve.

Note: Choose a combination of leaves – whatever is fresh and good on the day. Suggestions include rocket/arugula, young dandelion leaves, lamb's lettuce/corn-salad, flat-leaf parsley, baby spinach, sprigs of dill and nasturtium leaves.

INSALATA MISTA

If you ask for a mixed salad in Italy, this is what you will get. Don't be surprised if the tomatoes are not red and ripe, but hard and green – this is how they are eaten in salads. Salads do not come dressed – bottles of oil and vinegar are given to you so that you can dress your own.

350 g/12 oz. waxy salad
  potatoes
175 g/6 oz. fine green beans
extra virgin olive oil
50 g/¼ cup green olives,
  pitted
1 small crisp lettuce
2 large ripe tomatoes,
  quartered
3 tablespoons chopped fresh
  flat-leaf parsley
salt and freshly ground
  black pepper, to season

TO SERVE
extra virgin olive oil
red wine vinegar

SERVES 4

Peel the potatoes and boil in salted water for about 15 minutes, until tender, adding the beans 4 minutes before the potatoes are ready. Drain and cover with cold water to stop the cooking.

When cold, drain well. Transfer the beans to a bowl, slice the potatoes thickly and add to the beans, moistening with a little olive oil. Add the olives and toss well.

Wash the lettuce and tear into bite-size pieces. Add the lettuce and tomatoes to the potatoes and beans and toss lightly. Transfer to a serving bowl, season with salt and pepper and sprinkle over the parsley.

Dress with extra virgin olive oil and red wine vinegar and serve.

RESOURCES

UK

DeliVita
DeliVita.com
DeliVita is an innovative family-owned business that fuses British craftsmanship with Italian style and heritage to handcraft super luxe, wood-fired ovens in Yorkshire.

John Lewis
www.johnlewis.com
A brand of UK high-end department stores which stocks a wide range of excellent cookware, including pizza ovens, peels, fuel and all the other required accessories.

Lakeland
www.lakeland.co.uk
One of the UK's home shopping pioneers, offering an unrivalled collection of kitchenware and homeware.

Blue Diamond Garden Centre
www.bluediamond.gg
The second largest garden centre group in the UK and The Channel Islands, offering a huge variety of lifestyle products from plants to cookware.

Dobbies Garden Centres
www.dobbies.com
The biggest garden centre operator in the UK, stocking everything that a good garden needs and an excellent range of outdoor cooking products.

Burford Garden Centre
www.burford.co.uk
A famous Home and Garden Store in the heart of the Cotswolds in Oxfordshire. They sell first-rate outdoor cookware, including pizza ovens.

Divertimenti
www.divertimenti.co.uk
A food-lover's favourite since the 1960's, Divertimenti shops in South Kensington and London's West End stock an enormous range of cooking utensils and outdoor cookware.

Selfridge's
www.selfridges.com
A chain of high-end department stores in the United Kingdom, voted the best department store in the world. They stock pizza ovens amongst other outdoor cooking products.

Harrods
www.harrods.com
A famous department store in Knightsbridge, London, showcasing the finest products in food, fashion, homeware and technology, including pizza ovens and other outdoor cookware.

Alphin
www.alphin.co.uk
Professional online store for pizzerias and a fantastic source for the passionate pizza-maker.

Sous Chef
www.souschef.co.uk
Fantastic source of quality ingredients (including 'nduja) and cooking equipment.

US

Williams-Sonoma
www.williams-sonoma.com
Online cookshop with everything for home-baking and cooking, including round and square baking stones, wooden pizza peels and Bialetti pizza cutters.

West Elm
www.westelm.com
Sustainable home furnishings retailer offering modern furniture, home accessories and kitchenware.

Sur La Table
www.surlatable.com
'A second home for cooks' retailer selling kitchenware, housewares, food and outdoor products.

Home Depot
www.homedepot.com
The largest home improvement retailer in the US, supplying a variety of products including outdoor cookware.

Lowe's
www.lowes.com
American retail company specializing in home improvement, selling a range of outdoor cooking products amongst other items.

Bed Bath and Beyond
www.bedbathandbeyond.com
Chain of domestic merchandise retail stores, selling bedding, bathroom, kitchen products and home décor.

Dean & DeLuca

www.deandeluca.com
High-quality food and
kitchenware.

ChefShop.com

www.chefshop.com
Seattle-based website offering
a seasonal selection of more than
1,000 of the very best artisan-
produced foods and fresh
products from around the world.

King Arthur Flour

www.kingarthurflour.com
Vermont's venerable milling
company is an invaluable resource
for serious pizza-makers and
bread-bakers.

Caputo

www.caputoflour.com
'Flour of Naples', this producer
offers Italian '0' and '00' flours
from which to make pizza dough.

Penzeys

www.penzeys.com
Penzeys Spices offers more than
250 herbs, spices and seasonings,
including blue poppy seeds, white,
green or pink peppercorns, white
and green cardamom and
premium saffron.

'Nduja Artisans

www.ndujaartisans.com
Stockist listings for specialist
Italian ingredients, including
'nduja.

Eataly

www.eataly.com
A large Italian marketplace with
37 global locations including New
York, Chicago and London. Offers
a variety of restaurants, food and
beverage counters, bakery, retail
items and a cooking school.

INDEX

RECIPE CREDITS

All recipes by **Maxine Clark** with the following exceptions:

Valerie Aikman-Smith
Garden Herb Butter

Miranda Ballard
Homemade Mayonnaises

Fiona Beckett
Four Cheese Pizza

Ross Dobson
Fennel & Tomato Focaccia

Clare Ferguson
Black Olives Sott'Olio
Green Olives with Fennel
Insalata Di Campo

Ursula Ferrigno
Tomato & Mint Salad

Silvana Franco
Pizza Fiorentina

Liz Franklin
Black Grape Schiacciata

Carol Hilker
Spinach, Artichoke & Goats'
   Cheese Pizza

Jennifer Joyce
Sun-Blush Tomato Pesto
Roasted Tomatoes
Roasted Fennel
Caramelized Onions
Giardiniera

Jenny Linford
Triple Tomato Pizza
Roast Garlic Rosemary Focaccia
Cherry Tomato & Olive Focaccia

Jane Mason
Alpine Pizza

Louise Pickford
Chilli Oil & Garlic Oil

Isidora Popovic
Rustic Focaccia with Red Pepper
   & Onion

Annie Rigg
Mixed Pizzette Platter

PICTURE CREDITS

Jan Baldwin
Page 118

Steve Baxter
Page 64

Martin Brigdale
Pages 8 (bottom right) 22, 76, 84, 123

Peter Cassidy
Pages 4, 59, 60, 88, 99, 114, 115, 120

DeliVita
Pages 1, 8 (bottom left), 9 (top right), 10, 11, endpapers

Richard Jung
Pages 5, 6, 13, 14, 17, 18, 20, 21, 25, 26, 29, 30, 33, 34, 37, 40, 43, 45, 47, 48, 67, 68, 72, 75, 80, 87, 91, 92, 94, 96, 105, 125

Mowie Kay
Pages 9, 27, 38, 52, 55, 71, 101

William Lingwood
Page 33

Diana Miller
Pages 100, 109, 116

Steve Painter
Page 13

William Reavell
Page 8 (bottom middle)

Toby Scott
Pages 2, 51

Ian Wallace
Page 102

Kate Whitaker
Page 56

Clare Winfield
Pages 3, 83, 111, 112, 113